P9-BAW-991

JUL 2000

WHITE SOX
The Illustrated Story

by Richard Whittingham

Foreword by Frank Thomas
Introduction by Minnie Minoso

Quality Sports Publications

For information write:

Quality Sports Publications
24 Buysse Drive
Coal Valley, IL 61240
(309) 234-5016
(800) 464-1116

Duane Brown, Project Director
Melinda Brown, Designer
Susan Smith, Editor

Printed in the U.S.A.
by
Waslworth Publishing Co.
&
Dustjacket printed by
Richardson Printing, Inc.

ISBN 1-885758-09-X

**Right: Frank Thomas hits the last home run in
the old Comiskey Park, September 28, 1990.**
(Photo courtesy of *Photography By Schuth.*)

Dedication

This book celebrates a grand baseball history and a Chicago
legacy. Appropriately then, it is dedicated in particular to a coterie of devoted
Sox fans the author has had the pleasure of knowing – Mike
Herbert, Warren Hansen, Jim Maher, Mike Wrenn, John Wrenn, Tim Leahy
and Mike Lyons – and in general to the surrounding legion of fans
who have shared the various ecstasies, heartbreaks and
unending excitements of nearly 100 years of
White Sox baseball.

Acknowledgements

The author and publisher would especially like to thank the following
organizations for their help and cooperation in putting this book together:
the Chicago White Sox, especially owners Jerry Reinsdorf and Ed Einhorn,
Senior Vice President of Marketing and Broadcasting Rob Gallas,
Director of Marketing and Broadcasting Bob Grim and
Manager of Publications Suzanne Reichart;
the National Baseball Hall of Fame in Cooperstown, New York;
the Chicago Historical Society; and
Keith and Al Schuth with Photography by Schuth.

CONTENTS

Photo courtesy of *Photography By Schuth.*

Frank Thomas

1990 to Present

At the start of my first full season in Chicago in 1991, they were talking and writing about the White Sox being a team of promise. The ballclub was coming off a second-place finish in 1990, their best year since they won the American League West in '83. I felt proud to be joining a team with players like Carlton Fisk, Tim Raines, Robin Ventura, Ozzie Guillen and Jack McDowell, who were the forces behind the promise.

I only wanted to be part of that promise; I came with a burning desire to make it more than a promise; I wanted to be a real part of turning the promise into a reality. I think we are well on the way to doing that.

We came close in 1993, we were on our way there in 1994, and things are falling into place nicely now. It is our current and primary goal to reward the fans and ourselves with the reality of a World Series at Comiskey Park before the 20th century comes to a close. The White Sox fans, who are among the best and most loyal of any in the major leagues, deserve it.

We who have been blessed with the opportunity to play major-league baseball, owe much to the game and the fans who have so long supported it. I hope that we, in turn, can give back what has been given to us so generously. I try to give back to the fans through my dedication to the game and my play on the field, and also off the field through the Frank Thomas Charitable Foundation.

I truly feel today part of the White Sox promise. Keep watching, that promise is going to be a reality.

FOREWORD

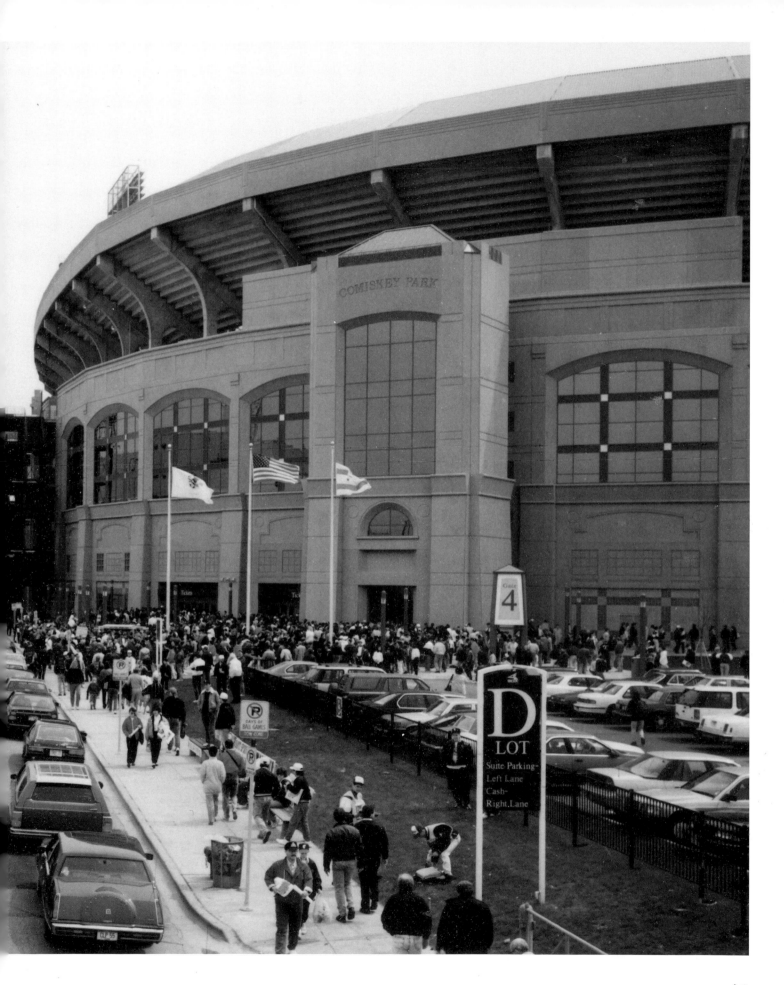

Minnie Minoso

1952-57, 1960-61, 1964, 1976 & 1980

The day I joined the White Sox is one I will always remember. May 1, 1951. It was the beginning of a new life for me, and Chicago and the White Sox have been a big part of it ever since.

I broke into the big leagues with the Cleveland Indians. I started the '51 season there, and I thought that was where my career was going to be. Al Lopez was the manager there and the Indians were a real pennant contender in those days (they finished in second place in 1951), but I was traded after only a few games, and I was very concerned about it.

I knew nothing really about Chicago. Except that neither the White Sox nor the Cubs had ever had a black player on their team before. I wondered how I would be received by my teammates, the fans, the organization. I remember I took the train to Chicago and was met at Union Station by some friends who knew me from the Negro Leagues. They took me to a room they were renting to me on the far south side of Chicago, and the next day I took the streetcar to Comiskey Park to make my first appearance.

I was put into the lineup, batting third, against the Yankees, the world champions. Eddie Robinson, our first baseman who was batting clean-up, gave me some advice and words of encouragement before I went to the plate. On the second pitch off Vic Raschi I hit the ball over the center field fence – what a heckuva way to start a career in Chicago. After that I never had to worry about the thoughts or feelings of my teammates or the fans. They were wonderful, and Chicago became the only town I could call my hometown.

My original teammates were the great "Go-Go" White Sox: Nellie Fox, Billy Pierce, Chico Carresquel and the others that followed. As I said in my autobiography, *Just Call Me Minnie,* "What a wonderful group of guys! What a talented bunch of athletes. A more amiable and unique group of ballplayers you will never find anywhere."

I enjoyed all the years I played for the "Go-Go" Sox in Chicago. The fans were great to me, and I loved them. Bill Veeck was wonderful back in those days. He was so special that no words can do him justice. He gave me nothing but respect and kindness, and I have never stopped appreciating what he did for me.

I left the White Sox, but I guess you could say my heart never did; and I, of course, came back to the team and the organization later.

For the last 16 years I have been associated with the White Sox front office, and I'm proud to be a member of that team.

I have been a very fortunate man. I was able to do the one thing I loved most, play big league baseball. I have had a great job on and off the field with the classiest organization in baseball, the White Sox ... and in a great city, Chicago.

INTRODUCTION

Photo courtesy of *Photography By Schuth.*

Prologue

Richard Whittingham

A captivating urban-landscape scene loomed in the stillness of
Chicago's South Side at dawn on a special day in White Sox lore, April
18, 1991. In the daybreaking sun that edged above Lake Michigan to
the east stood a stark portrait in contrast, divided by the slash of 35th
Street: to the south rose the gleaming new and as yet unbaptized
Comiskey Park, awaiting the opening-day crowd; to the north was
the shell of the moribund old Comiskey Park, awaiting only the final
ravages of the wrecker's ball and the bulldozers.

The day heralded the beginning of a new era in the White Sox
story.

Six and a half months earlier, the situation ironically was in exact
reverse. On September 30, 1990, it was the old stadium that stood
resolute, proud and intact, awaiting the arrival of the final-day crowd,
while across 35th Street the new stadium sat empty and incomplete.
That day, too, was quite special to White Sox fans because it signalled
the end of an era, the last game to be played in the venerable old stadium
known as Comiskey Park (the oldest in the major leagues at the time)
where, every year without fail, despite world wars and punishing
economic depressions, the ballclub had hosted its fans for more than
eight decades since its gates were first opened back on July 1, 1910.

That final day... It is best captured in the words of a legendary Sox
fan by the name of Mike Herbert who had been attending games there
since the late 1940s: "It was sunny and warm, maybe 70 degrees, a
beautiful day for a ballgame. The people began arriving around ten in

the morning, even though the gates wouldn't open until eleven, and they were just milling about outside the ballpark. There were families, some even three generations – grandparents, parents, kids. But it wasn't like an ordinary baseball crowd. There wasn't the noise and bustle. The people were hushed, almost reverent, like you'd see in a church or a museum, and that carried over after we all filed into the stadium; it was like nothing I'd ever seen at a baseball game before. It was as if we'd come to say goodbye forever to a good friend. And, of course, we had."

No one was saying goodbye to the White Sox, however; just to the friendly home that had become old and dated. It was time. So the team, the organization and the fans simply moved across the street into a modernized, 21st century residence, and once again went about the business of playing baseball.

It was a fitting way to begin the last decade of the 20th century – with a freshness and a revitalized sense of hope. The White Sox, after all, began the centenary with more than promise and hope. They walked away with the very first American League pennant in 1901. Midway through that first decade, they won their first World Series defeating the Cubs in 1906, four games to two, in what remains Chicago's only intra-city baseball world championship match.

During the century, there have been countless Sox moments to remember and a wonderful and colorful parade of players and personalities who have brought special honor to the various White Sox uniforms they wore.

During the first half of the 1900s, there were such memorable Hall of Fame enshrinees as Big Ed Walsh, Eddie Collins, Ray Schalk, Red Faber, Harry Hooper, Ted Lyons and Luke Appling. Short of the Hall honor, but still stars of earned magnitude, were such other Sox greats as Frank Isbell, Shoeless Joe Jackson, Eddie Cicotte, Buck Weaver, Johnny Mostil, Happy Felsch, Earl Sheely, Bibb Falk, Zeke Bonura, Rip Radcliff, Monty Stratton, Eddie Lopat, Pat Seerey, Cass Michaels, Dave Philley, Taffy Wright and Bill Wight.

The 1950s introduced us to Nellie Fox, Chico Carrasquel, Gus Zernial, Eddie Robinson, Billy Pierce, Minnie Minoso, Jim Rivera, Sherm Lollar, Saul Rogovin, Walt Dropo, George Kell, Dick Donovan, Larry Doby, Jim Landis and Early Wynn.

In the 1960s, we saw such Sox stellars as Al Smith, Floyd Robinson, Juan Pizarro, Gary Peters, Luis Aparicio, Pete Ward, Joel Horlen, Hoyt Wilhelm, Moose Skowron, Eddie Fisher and Tommy McCraw.

The 1970s brought us luminaries the likes of Wilbur Wood, Bill Melton, Walt Williams, Dick Allen, Carlos May, Jim Kaat, Jorge Orta, Ralph Garr, Ed Herrmann, Lamar Johnson, Terry Forster, Goose Gossage, Bucky Dent, Chet Lemon, Ken Kravec and Steve Stone.

For the decade of the '80s, there was Greg Luzinski, Britt Burns, Harold Baines, Rich Dotson, LaMarr Hoyt, Ron Kittle, Carlton Fisk, Greg Walker, Floyd Bannister, Ivan Calderon and Bobby Thigpen.

The 1990s – the decade of promise and hope – it has already offered Ozzie Guillen, Jack McDowell, Tim Raines, Robin Ventura, Lance Johnson, Alex Fernandez, Ron Karkovice, Wilson Alvarez, Dave Martinez, Roberto Hernandez, Frank Thomas, Albert Belle and Harold Baines again.

It has been a long and illustrious baseball history.

If there was a reverence at the passing of the old Comiskey Park and a fresh hope that characterized the birth of the new one, it will be interesting to see the cornucopia of emotions that a successful pennant race and a World Series appearance will invoke in the White Sox faithful.

To end the 20th century as triumphantly as the White Sox began it, that is the supplication of Sox fans everywhere.

Photo courtesy of *Photography By Schuth*

Where it all began: South Side Park at 39th and Wentworth, the first home of the Chicago White Sox.

1

The Early Years

The White Sox came to Chicago with the turn of the century. In 1900, William McKinley was president of the United States and Carry Nation was storming saloons with her hatchet in hand. It was the year of only the second modern Olympic Games and a mere 10 years since Dr. James Naismith had invented the game of basketball. There was no NFL, NBA, NCAA or NHL. James J. Jeffries was the heavyweight champion of the world. Red Grange, Bobby Jones and Jesse Owens hadn't even been born, and Jack Dempsey, Bill Tilden and Paavo Nurmi were just little boys who had yet to start to school.

In the first month of the 20th century, Charles A. Comiskey, owner and manager of a minor league franchise in St. Paul, brought his club from Minnesota to the city of Chicago to join the newly formed American League. The new baseball league was the brainchild of Ban Johnson, the president of the minors' Western League. He wanted to launch another major league, one to compete on the same ground as the well-established National League.

In 1900, however, his league was still minor. But it was well-organized. Besides Chicago, AL teams had homes in Milwaukee, Indianapolis, Detroit, Kansas City, Cleveland, Buffalo and Minneapolis. And the owners of all of the teams had their collective eye on playing *major* league baseball very soon.

The White Sox were known as the "White Stockings" back then and

THE FIRST AMERICAN LEAGUE GAME
April 24, 1901, at Chicago

Cleveland Blues

Ollie Pickering	rf
Jack McCarthy	lf
Frank Genins	cf
Candy LaChance	1b
Bill Bradley	3b
Erve Beck	2b
Bill Hallman	ss
Bob Wood	c
Bill Hoffer	p
Mgr: Jimmy McAleer	

Chicago White Stockings

Dummy Hoy	cf
Fielder Jones	rf
Sam Mertes	lf
Frank Shugart	ss
Frank Isbell	1b
Fred Hartman	3b
Dave Brain	2b
Billy Sullivan	c
Roy Patterson	p
Mgr: Clark Griffith	

Clark Griffith defected from the National League in 1901 to manage and pitch for the White Sox in the neophyte American League. He led them to a pennant that first year and at the same time hurled 24 wins while losing only 7 games. Griffith would go on to manage and pitch for the Yankees and the Senators, eventually to be enshrined in the Hall of Fame.

their ballpark was on the old Chicago Cricket Club grounds at 39th and Wentworth. Their debut at that park was April 21, 1900, and 5,200 fans came out to watch them. They lost 5-4 in 10 innings to a Milwaukee team managed by Connie Mack. But they went on to win 82 games that inaugural year against 53 losses (.607), enough to earn the first American League Championship. (They ended up four games ahead of the second-place Milwaukee club.) The most remarkable performance of the year was the four straight shutouts by White Stocking pitcher Jack Katoll, all identical 3-0 wins.

The American became a major league the following year and from that moment on, Chicago was home to two big league franchises. There were eight teams in each major league in 1901, and although the AL was indeed a reality, there would be no World Series until 1903.

Many of the stars of the NL defected to the fledgling AL that first year. Chicago enticed 31-year-old Clark Griffith to take the mound for them and to manage the team. Other greats who abandoned the nationals included Cy Young, Nap Lajoie, John McGraw and Iron Man Joe McGinnity. Still, the National League kept such name players as Christy Mathewson, Rube Waddell, Kid Nichols, Wild Bill Donovan, Wee Willie Keeler, Ed Delahanty, Frank Chance, Jesse

The first American League pennant winners, the 1901 White Sox. Left to right: Back row – Patterson, Burke, Jones, Sugden; Third row – Foster, Piatt, Katoll, Isbell, Mertes, Hartman; Second row – Griffith, Comiskey, Callahan; First row – Sullivan, Hoy, mascot, Shugart, McFarland.

Burkett, and Sam Crawford.

The White Stockings gained the distinction of having played the first game in American League history, an honor they would have been forced to share had the games scheduled for Baltimore, Detroit and Philadelphia not been rained out that day. In Chicago, however, the sun shone on April 24th and the American League was launched before 14,000 fans out on Chicago's South Side. There was music from the Rough Riders Band, the ceremony of throwing out the first ball, and the announcement that the team's name was being abbreviated to "White Sox."

The White Sox won the pennant that maiden year of the American League. Clark Griffith posted 24 victories for them and lost only seven games. Roy Patterson was another 20-game winner. Fielder Jones, who played right field, led the team with a .311 batting average and third baseman Fred Hartman was only two percentage points behind him. First baseman Frank Isbell stole 52 bases, the most in either league that year, and the team themselves – perhaps the original "Go-Go" Sox – led the majors with a total of 280 base thefts. When the season ended, the White Sox had a record of 83-53 (.610), four games in front of the runners-up from Boston.

Nixey Callahan pitched the first no-hit game in White Sox history on September 20, 1902, beating Detroit 3-0.

Cy Young won 33 games for Boston in the AL that year, the most in either league. And Nap Lajoie of Philadelphia was the first AL triple crown winner, batting .422, hitting 14 homers, and driving in 125 runs. After it was over, there was little doubt that the American League would be able to live comfortably and profitably with the older National League, who as a result of the trespass of the AL had rather joylessly celebrated its 25th anniversary.

Life at the top was short for the Sox, however. They dropped to fourth place in 1902 and plummeted to seventh the following year. Griffith departed the team just before the 1903 season to go to New York and manage a new franchise that was to become known as the Yankees. Although they were declining, the Sox were still exciting to watch: a base-stealing team with one of the finest fielding units in the league. They just couldn't hit very well. Fielder Jones and Danny Green were the only consistent hitters, near or above .300. As for slugging in those years, the most the team as a whole could produce in one season was 14 home runs.

Left: Guy "Doc" White came to the Sox in 1903 and remained a pitching mainstay for the next 10 years. A reedy 6'1", 150-pounder, he led the league in 1906 with an ERA of 1.52. But his best year was 1907 when he won 25 games for the Sox and lost only 13.

In 1904, Doc White pitched five consecutive shutouts, a major league record that would not be broken until Don Drysdale hurled six straight shutouts for the Los Angeles Dodgers in 1968.

Doc White became a member of the Sox pitching staff in 1902, Nick Altrock and Frank Owen joined him in 1903, and Big Ed Walsh arrived in 1904. All would engrave their names on early White Sox pitching records. Another hurler, Patsy Flaherty, would earn the ignoble distinction in 1903 of being the first Sox pitcher to lose more than 20 games in a season (his record, 11-25).

The White Sox and the Cubs played their first interleague series in 1903, a 14-game affair held after the regular season. Chicago baseball fans of either persuasion equally shared the joys and woes of it as the Sox and Cubs won seven games each. It would be an autumn tradition that would not come to an end until the war years of the 1940s.

By 1904, the Sox were on their way back up – to third place anyway – on the arms of 21-game winners Nick Altrock and Frank Owen, and 16-game winners Frank Smith and Doc White, as well as some very fleet feet on the basepaths (the team's 216 thefts were the league high, and no less than 10 players stole 11 bases or more). Fielder Jones had taken over the managerial tasks midway through the season, although he still held court in center field as well. Ed Walsh in his rookie season was relatively unimpressive, with a 5-5 record, but Old Roman Comiskey said he had "great faith in that young man's potential."

It was not until 1906 that the Sox returned to the top. The year before, they made a strong bid for the pennant, narrowly losing out in the closing days of the season to a Philadelphia team whose fortunes had been guided by two devastating pitchers, Rube Waddell and Eddie Plank. The next year, however, it would be a story with a happier ending for Sox fans.

They were called the "Hitless Wonders," those White Sox of 1906, but they managed to win the American League pennant with a record of 93-58 (.616) despite a team batting average of .230 and a slugging average of .286, both being the lowest in the league. The Sox hit only six home runs the entire year, and Fielder Jones was the club's premier slugger with two roundtrippers.

Still they were there, the AL representative in baseball's third World Series. It would come to be called the "Trolley Series" because it was played in one city and fans could commute back and forth between the Cubs' West Side Park and the Sox field on the south side via Chicago's venerable trolley cars. It also would come to stand as Chicago's only intra-city World Series.

The Cubs were a heavy favorite. They had won a grand total of 116 games in 1906 and lost only 36 (.763). Both records – most wins and highest win percentage in a season – still stand today. They had the famous infield combination of Joe Tinker, Johnny Evers and Frank Chance. They boasted a pitching staff which included Mordecai "Three Finger" Brown, Ed Reulbach and Jack Pfiester, who won 65 games among them. The Cubs' team batting average of .262 was 32 percentage points higher than that of the Sox.

Frank Smith hurled no-hit baseball for the White Sox on September 6, 1905, blanking the Detroit Tigers 15-0. Three years later he would pitch another against the Philadelphia Athletics, 1-0, and become the only pitcher in Sox history to hurl two no-hit games. He also posted two one-hitters in 1905.

The White Sox set an American League record in 1906 when they won 19 consecutive games without a loss. The streak began August 2nd and lasted through August 23rd, during which the Sox outscored their opponents 100-24. There was also a 0-0 tie. The record win streak still stands but was tied by the New York Yankees in 1947.

Left: Fielder Jones joined the White Sox outfield in 1901, then took over as manager in 1904. He led the Sox to a pennant (1906) after a second-place finish the year before. He was acknowledged as one of the game's finest strategists in those early days of the American League.

Right: Owner Charles A. "Old Roman" Comiskey is caricatured here before the flag symbolizing the pennant and World Series championship his White Sox gained for Chicago in 1906. Founder of the Sox and an instrumental figure in the birth and development of the American League, Comiskey was inducted into the Hall of Fame in 1939.

WORLD SERIES – 1906				
Game	**R**	**H**	**E**	**Pitchers**
Game 1				
Sox	2	4	1	Nick Altrock
Cubs	1	4	2	Three Finger Brown
Game 2				
Cubs	7	10	2	Ed Reulbach
Sox	1	1	2	Doc White, Frank Owen
Game 3				
Sox	3	4	1	Ed Walsh
Cubs	0	2	2	Jack Pfeister
Game 4				
Cubs	1	7	1	Three Finger Brown
Sox	0	2	1	Nick Altrock
Game 5				
Sox	8	12	6	Ed Walsh, Doc White
Cubs	6	6	0	Ed Reulbach, Jack Pfeister, Orvie Overall
Game 6				
Cubs	3	8	0	Three Finger Brown, Orvie Overall
Sox	8	14	3	Doc White

The World Series champs of 1906, the team that defeated the Chicago Cubs in the only intra-city World Series ever played in Chicago. Left to right: Front row – Babe Towne, Nick Altrock, Frank Owen, Roy Patterson, Patsy Dougherty, Fielder Jones, Lou Fiene. Middle row – Ed Walsh, Frank Smith, Frank Roth, Ed Hahn, August Dundon, John Donohue, Lee Tannehill, Bill O'Neill, George Rohe. Top row – Hub Hart, Ed McFarland, George Davis, Charles Comiskey, Frank Isbell, Bill Sullivan, Doc White.

But baseball is unpredictable and the 1906 Series certainly was a cogent example of that. Everything was unexplainably juxtaposed. Suddenly there was a Cub team that could not hit and a Sox team that could. It took six games for the White Sox to win it, and in the last two the once-weak Sox offense scored eight runs in each game and knocked out a total of 26 hits in the two slugfests. Big Ed Walsh won two games (one a shutout), and Nick Altrock and Doc White got wins in the other two. There was another factor as well: the managerial acumen of Fielder Jones who, as one writer of the day put it, "made all the right decisions and none of the wrong ones."

When it was over, there was little question that Walsh had emerged as the team's premier pitcher. A big man, especially in those days (6'1", 220 pounds), he would reinforce his pitching reputation the following year with 24 wins and a league-leading ERA of 1.60. To say Walsh was an iron man on the mound is an understatement. He

Big Ed Walsh was the premier White Sox pitcher from 1906 through 1912. He chalked up two wins in the 1906 World Series, but the high point of his career was the 40 wins he posted in 1908. He was inducted into the Hall of Fame in 1946.

pitched and won both games of a double-header in 1908, and in 1907 and 1908 he pitched in 56 and 66 games respectively, often with no more than two days' rest. In 1908, he won 40 games, by far the most in White Sox history.

The Sox, however, were not as lustrous as Walsh in the years that followed their World Series victory. They dropped to third place in 1907 and 1908, then to fourth, and finally sixth, as the Detroit Tigers, behind the hitting of Ty Cobb and Sam Crawford, and the pitching of Wild Bill Donovan and George Mullin, came to dominate the American League in the second half of the century's first decade.

Pitching and fielding were not Sox problems in those years. In fact the team often led the league in those categories. Hitting was the real void. In 1908, the team hit only *three* home runs all season, a major league low which never has and surely never will be removed from the record books. In 1909, they hit four, and the following year zoomed to seven. The team batting average was as low as .211, and at best was only .237 (1907). Fans remained loyal, however, and in 1907 alone the Sox led both leagues in home attendance (666,307).

At the end of the decade, the Sox got a new home. The stadium was built on the corner of 35th and Shields. For $100,000, Old Roman Comiskey had bought a 600x600 foot lot from the estate of Chicago's first mayor, John Wentworth. Formal groundbreaking was held in the middle of February 1909, and the first game was played on July 1, 1910. The architect was Zachary Taylor Davis, who would later design Wrigley Field as well, and his plans called for a seating capacity of 35,000 – 6,400 box seats, 12,600 grandstand seats, and wooden-bench bleachers to accommodate 16,000. The original dimensions were 362 feet along each foul line and a long 420 feet to dead center field. The cost of construction was somewhere in the vicinity of $500,000. It was formally called White Sox Park; Comiskey's name would not be inscribed on it until later in the decade.

New stadium or not, the Sox remained a mediocre ballclub for the next six years. It was 1916 before there was anything that could be described as pennant fever on Chicago's South Side. Since Fielder Jones had retired from managing the Sox in 1908, the club had gone through three managers – Billy Sullivan, Hugh Duffy and Nixey Callahan – but the team still went steadily down during those years (1909-1914). Clarence "Pants" Rowland took over in 1915 and the tide was jarringly reversed. He managed to take a sixth-place team with a won-loss percentage of .455, which had ended up 30 games out at the end of the season, and turn it into a third-place team with a .604 winning percentage, which trailed the league-leading Boston Red Sox by only 9 1/2 games.

Before Pants Rowland arrived, however, the Sox made some of the most propitious acquisitions in the team's history. First, they purchased

FIRST GAME
COMISKEY PARK
July 1, 1910

Chicago White Sox

Charlie French	2b
George Browne	cf
Shano Collins	rf
Bruno Block	c
Patsy Dougherty	lf
Chick Gandil	1b
Billy Purtell	3b
Lena Blackburne	ss
Ed Walsh	p

Mgr: Hugh Duffy

St. Louis Browns

George Stone	lf
Roy Hartzell	3b
Bobby Wallace	ss
Pat Newnam	1b
Al Schweitzer	cf
Danny Hoffman	rf
Frank Truesdale	2b
Bill Killefer	c
Barney Pelty	p

Mgr: Jack O'Connor

The first home run hit in Comiskey Park was by Lee Tannehill of the Sox, a utility infielder, against the Detroit Tigers (August 1, 1910) a full month after baseball had come to the new stadium. It was Tannehill's only homer of the year, a grand slammer, and one of the only seven hit by White Sox players during the entire season.

On tour with the White Sox, 1913. The player with the little girl is Big Ed Walsh. (Depicted on a postcard.)

Ed Walsh pitched his first and only no-hit game for the White Sox August 27, 1911, a 5-0 win over the Boston Red Sox.

BIG ED WALSH'S CAREER WITH THE WHITE SOX

Year	Won	Lost	ERA	SO's
1904	6	3	2.60	57
1905	8	3	2.17	71
1906	17	13	1.88	171
1907	24	18	1.60	206
1908	40	15	1.42	269
1909	15	11	1.41	127
1910	18	20	1.27	258
1911	27	18	2.22	255
1912	27	17	2.15	254
1913	8	3	2.58	34
1914	2	3	2.82	15
1915	3	0	1.33	12
1916	0	1	2.70	3
Career	**195**	**125**	**1.82**	**1,732**

the services of pitcher Eddie Cicotte from the Red Sox. Then came catcher Ray "Cracker" Schalk from the Milwaukee minor league club. In 1913, Urban "Red" Faber was brought up from Des Moines. And the infield jewel, Ed "Cocky" Collins, destined to be one of the game's greatest stars, signed on after the 1914 season.

By 1915, the White Sox actually could boast of a team hitting threat. Eddie Collins batted .332 that year, second only in the AL to Ty Cobb's .369. In addition, Sox first baseman Jack Fournier hit .322, third-best in the AL, and his slugging average of .491 was highest in the league. The Sox team total of 25 home runs was second-best.

The following year the White Sox stayed in the thick of the pennant race all the way to the wire, only to lose out in the final days to the Boston Red Sox. (The pennant winners of 1916 were spurred by a pitcher named Babe Ruth who won 23 games for them and led the league with an ERA of 1.75.) For the White Sox, three batters hit above .300. Shoeless Joe Jackson, who had been acquired from Cleveland the season before, led the team with .341, trailing only Tris

Ewell "Reb" Russell set a major league record for shutouts pitched by a rookie in 1913. His eight scoreless wins that year still stand in the record books. (The record was tied in 1981 by Fernando Valenzuela of the Los Angeles Dodgers.) Russell also won 22 and lost 16 his freshman year in the American League.

Ray Schalk signed with the White Sox in 1912 and was the starting catcher for the next decade and a half. A diminutive backstop (5'9", 165 lbs.), his fiery hustle earned him the nickname "Cracker," and he was, in the words of sportswriter Dave Condon, "as fine a fellow as ever drew on the White Sox flannels." Schalk also was a great enough ballplayer to earn entrance into the Hall of Fame. He caught in 1,755 games for the Sox and had a career batting average of .253. (Photo courtesy of the National Baseball Hall of Fame.)

One of the all-time great White Sox pitchers, Urban "Red" Faber was the Sox ace from 1914 through the 1920s. In Sox history, only Ted Lyons won more games for the Sox. Faber won more than 20 games in a season four times; his best effort was in 1921 when he won 25 and lost 15, posting an ERA of 2.48. Faber was inducted into the Hall of Fame in 1964. His career stats: 254 wins, 213 losses; 669 games, 4,087.2 innings pitched, and a career ERA of 3.15.

Red Faber threw a mere 67 pitches in a nine-inning game against Washington, May 12, 1915. He allowed only three hits, and in two innings retired the side on three pitches each. Faber also won eight straight games that year on his way to a 24-14 season.

RED FABER'S CAREER WITH THE WHITE SOX

Year	Won	Lost	ERA	SO's
1914	10	9	2.68	88
1915	24	14	2.55	182
1916	17	9	2.02	87
1917	16	13	1.92	84
1918*	4	1	1.23	26
1919	11	9	3.83	45
1920	23	13	2.99	108
1921	25	15	2.48	124
1922	21	17	2.80	148
1923	14	11	3.41	91
1924**	9	11	3.85	47
1925	12	11	3.78	71
1926	15	9	3.56	65
1927**	4	7	4.55	39
1928	13	9	3.75	43
1929	13	13	3.88	68
1930	8	13	4.21	62
1931	10	14	3.82	49
1932	2	11	3.74	26
1933	3	4	3.44	18
Lifetime	**254**	**213**	**3.15**	**1,471**

*In military service most of the season
**Hampered much of the season with an injured arm

Speaker (.386) and Ty Cobb (.371) in the AL. Eddie Collins hit .308 and Oscar "Happy" Felsch came in at a respectable .300 in his sophomore year in the major leagues. Shoeless Joe also led the majors in triples with 21, a White Sox team record which still stands today.

But it was 1917 that was destined to be the year of the White Sox. Babe Ruth's pitching (24-13) could not get the Red Sox higher than second place, and the respective hitting of Speaker (.352) and Cobb (.383) could not bring the Athletics and the Tigers any higher than third and fourth place. The Sox galloped through the league that year; the nearest to their dust was a full nine games back at season's end. Their 100 wins that year is the most a White Sox team has ever posted in a season. With only 54 losses, their .649 percentage is another all-time club high. Cicotte won 28 games for the Sox and his ERA of 1.53 was the league's best. Hitting was consistent, with Happy Felsch high at .308 and Jackson next with .301.

It would be John "Little Napoleon" McGraw's New York Giants whom the White Sox would have to face in the World Series of 1917. They too had breezed through their league with a 98-56 record and a 10-game margin at the end of the season. Big names were not the forte of the Giants, although they had a pinch hitter named Jim

1914 pitching: Jim Scott pitched no-hit ball for nine innings, only to see his no-hitter go down the drain in the 10th when Chick Gandil of Washington singled. (Gandil would later be traded to the White Sox and become a major figure in the infamous "Black Sox" scandal.) Two weeks later, Sox pitcher Joe Benz pitched a no-hitter, defeating the Indians 6-1.

These marchers are Chicago White Sox players, appearing at Comiskey Park in 1917. It was a patriotic pre-game ceremony and afterwards the players changed uniforms and played baseball. During the following year, however, most of them would be in a military uniform full-time or working in industry for the war effort.

Clarence "Pants" Rowland was the only Sox manager ever to win 100 games in a season, a feat he accomplished in 1917 as he was guiding the team to a pennant and a World Series championship. Rowland took the White Sox from a sixth-place team in 1914 directly up the American League ladder: third, second, then a pennant. Guiding the Sox over four years he won 339 games and lost 247 (.578).

Ed Cicotte pitched a no-hitter for the Sox on April 14, 1917, shutting out the St. Louis Browns 11-0.

Game	R	H	E	Pitchers
WORLD SERIES – 1917				
Game 1				
Giants	1	7	1	Slim Sallee
Sox	2	7	1	Ed Cicotte
Game 2				
Giants	2	8	1	Ferdie Schupp, Fred Anderson Pol Perritt, Jeff Tesreau
Sox	7	14	1	Red Faber
Game 3				
Sox	0	5	3	Ed Cicotte
Giants	2	8	2	Rube Benton
Game 4				
Sox	0	7	0	Red Faber, Dave Danforth
Giants	5	10	1	Ferdie Schupp
Game 5				
Giants	5	12	3	Slim Sallee, Pol Perritt
Sox	8	14	6	Reb Russell, Ed Cicotte, Lefty Williams, Red Faber
Game 6				
Sox	4	7	1	Red Faber
Giants	2	6	3	Rube Benton, Pol Perritt

Thorpe who would immortalize himself in other sports. What the Giants did have was consistency, power, and speed (they led the NL in runs scored, home runs, and stolen bases).

The nation was at war when the two teams went head to head for the world championship of baseball in 1917. Still, the fans came out in record numbers. The White Sox won the first game 2-1, at home behind the masterful pitching of Eddie Cicotte, and took a two-game lead the next day. But at the Polo Grounds, the Giants took advantage of the home field and shut the Sox out in the next two games. Back at Comiskey Park, the Sox came from behind to win Game Five and take a 3-2 lead in the Series. The sixth game was back at the Polo Grounds, and the Giants could never overcome the three runs they gave up in the fourth inning. One of them they truly gave away when Eddie Collins, trapped on third base, found that in the rundown no one was covering home plate and raced in to register a run scored instead of a crucial out. The final score was 4-2. It was the second world championship for the White Sox in two trips to the World Series.

1918 was a year the majors might just as well have forgotten. The ranks of players were grandly depleted by the loss of men going to war or to work in industry for the war effort. The Sox lost Shoeless Joe Jackson, Red Faber, Happy Felsch, Swede Risberg and Lefty Williams from their pennant-winning starting lineup. The Sox only played 124 games that year in an abbreviated season, and the team came in sixth with a record of 57-67.

The next year everybody was back; everybody, that is, except Pants Rowland. He turned the managership over to William "Kid" Gleason. The team was awesome, considered by many as the finest in White Sox history. The team batting average of .287 set a club record for the 20-year-old franchise and was the highest in both leagues that year. The Sox also scored the most runs and collected the most hits in the majors, and stole the most bases in the AL. Eddie Cicotte was baseball's ranking pitcher, with a record of 29-7 (.806). His number of wins, winning percentage, and total innings pitched (307) were major league highs in 1919.

Eddie Cicotte began pitching in the major leagues in 1905; he pitched for the White Sox starting in 1913. His best years were the last four of his career, 1917-1920. In three of those he won 29, 28 and 21 games. But Cicotte was one of the infamous "Black Sox" and he was expelled from baseball in 1920. His lifetime stats: 208 wins, 149 losses; 502 games, 3,224.1 innings pitched; and an ERA of 2.37.

The Sox were odds-on favorites to defeat a nondescript Cincinnati Reds team in the 1919 World Series. But, as every baseball fan knows, they didn't. In an experimental World Series, upped to the best of nine games, they lost the championship to the Reds five games to three. It was a stunning upset, but not nearly as stunning as the revelation that would come almost a year later – that it had not indeed been a valid upset. The Series had been fixed; seven White Sox players had thrown it for a reported $100,000 from a group of gamblers.

Above: Buck Weaver was the Sox shortstop and sometimes third baseman from 1912 through 1920. He was one of the eight "Black Sox" banned for life after the 1919 World Series scandal, although it later was proved that he had not taken part in the fix, only knew about it. Weaver had his best year with the Sox in 1920 when he was batting .333 before being ousted from baseball.

Above: Kid Gleason rapped a few fungoes here to his White Sox team of 1919, the year he took over as manager. He guided the Sox to a pennant that year but, betrayed by some of his players, lost the World Series to the Cincinnati Reds five games to three. Gleason had pitched and played second base in the majors from 1888 to 1912. He managed the Sox through 1923, winning 392 and losing 364 (.519). (Photo courtesy of the *Chicago Historical Society.*)

WORLD SERIES - 1919

Game	R	H	E	Pitchers
Game 1				
Sox	1	6	1	Ed Cicotte, Roy Wilkinson, Grover Lowdermilk
Reds	9	14	1	Dutch Ruether
Game 2				
Sox	2	10	1	Lefty Williams
Reds	4	4	2	Slim Sallee
Game 3				
Reds	0	3	1	Ray Fisher, Dolf Luque
Sox	3	7	0	Dickie Kerr
Game 4				
Reds	2	5	2	Jimmy Ring
Sox	0	3	2	Ed Cicotte
Game 5				
Reds	5	4	0	Hod Eller
Sox	0	3	3	Lefty Williams, Erskine Mayer
Game 6				
Sox	5	10	3	Dickie Kerr
Reds	4	11	0	Dutch Ruether, Jimmy Ring
Game 7				
Sox	4	10	1	Ed Cicotte
Reds	1	7	4	Slim Sallee, Ray Fisher, Dolf Luque
Game 8				
Reds	10	16	2	Hod Eller
Sox	5	10	1	Lefty Williams, Bill James, Roy Wilkinson

Chick Gandil is called out as he slides into second during a game in the infamous World Series of 1919. Gandil, the Sox first baseman since 1917, was alleged to be one of the chief liaisons between the gamblers and the players in the "Black Sox" scandal.

There were suspicions early on that everything had not been right; rumors abounded that some hanky-panky had been going on. Old Roman Comiskey offered a $10,000 reward to anyone who could produce some solid evidence that his ballplayers had done anything illegal to affect the outcome of the Series. He even held up payment of the players' share of the World Series gate for six months.

The evidence was finally brought to light in September 1920. A group of Pittsburgh gamblers, suspecting they were on the bum end of a double-cross in another betting situation, let word out that the previous year's Series had been fixed. A grand jury was called in Chicago and a thorough investigation followed. Witness after witness was called and on September 26, two Sox superstars, Eddie Cicotte and Shoeless Joe Jackson, broke down and confessed that they had indeed thrown the Series.

The story has been told countless times: As Shoeless Joe Jackson walked out of the courthouse a little boy with tear-filled eyes ran up to him and pleaded, "Say it ain't so, Joe." But it was. Before it was over, eight players were implicated. Besides Shoeless Joe and Eddie Cicotte, first baseman Chick Gandil (the alleged ringleader), shortstop Swede Risberg, center fielder Happy Felsch, pitcher Lefty Williams, infielder Fred McMullin, and third baseman Buck Weaver were suspended from the game of baseball for life by Judge Kenesaw Landis, commissioner of baseball. Later it was proved that Weaver had not been in on the deal but had known about it. All the same, he paid the identical price as his cohorts.

As it turned out, the errant players had collected less than half the $100,000 they were supposed to have received, and the White Sox of 1919 were dubbed forever the "Black Sox."

Shoeless Joe Jackson, the most famous of those caught up in the "Black Sox" scandal, was one of the greatest hitters ever to play major league baseball. His career batting average of .356 is third-best in major league history, exceeded only by Ty Cobb (.367) and Rogers Hornsby (.358). His career high was .408 in 1911.

Shoeless Joe Jackson set the all-time White Sox record for total bases in 1920 – 336. He collected 74 extra base hits – 12 home runs, 20 triples and 42 doubles – and 144 singles.

SHOELESS JOE JACKSON'S CAREER WITH THE WHITE SOX

Year	Batting Average	2B	3B	HR	RBIs
1915	.265	4	5	2	36
1916	.341	40	21	3	78
1917	.301	20	17	5	75
1918*	.354	2	2	1	20
1919	.351	31	14	7	96
1920	.382	42	20	12	121
Career	**.339**	**139**	**79**	**30**	**426**

*Out most of the season to work in industrial war effort.

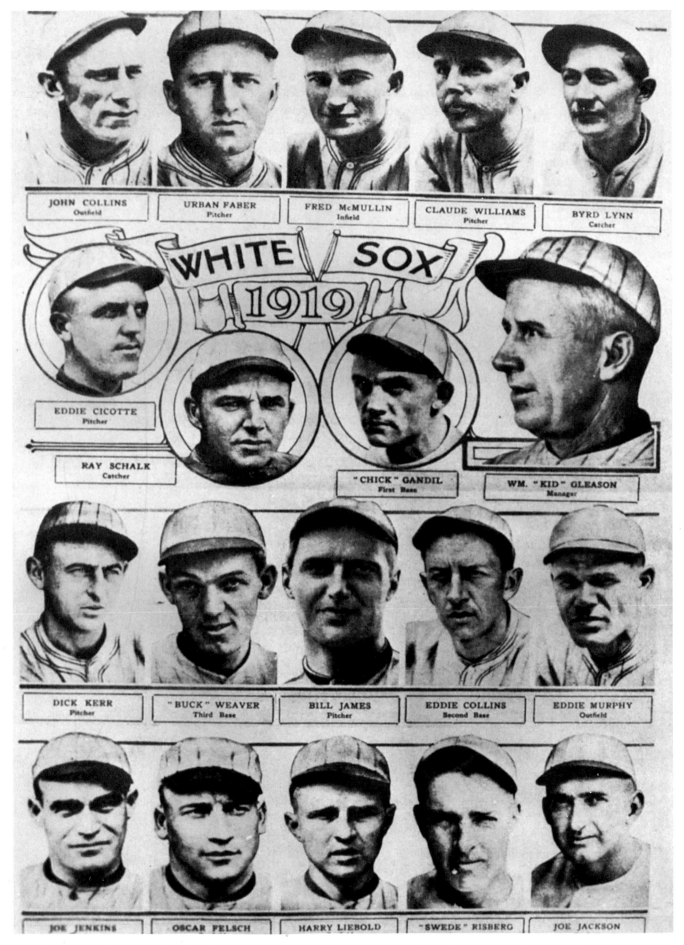

The White Sox of 1919. Those whose Sox turned "Black" were: Shoeless Joe Jackson, Eddie Cicotte, Chick Gandil, Lefty Williams, Happy Felsch, Fred McMullin, Swede Risberg and Buck Weaver.

The White Sox had been a strong contender for the 1920 American League pennant because they were able to play almost the entire season with the talent that would in September be expelled from the game. They were in a neck-and-neck pennant race with Cleveland, managed by Tris Speaker, but the Sox world fell apart with the revelation of the scandal. They finished second, two games behind the Indians. Shoeless Joe was hitting .382, Happy Felsch .338, and Buck Weaver .333 when they were ousted; Cicotte had won 21 games and Lefty Williams 22.

The White Sox were badly soiled in spirit by the scandal of 1919, and the roster was obviously stripped of much of its store of talent. In the first 20 years of the club's existence, only five times had the Sox ended their season outside the first division. But in 1921, they descended into the second division and would not emerge from the depths of it for the next 15 years. And it would take four decades before they would entertain another World Series.

Outfielder Oscar "Happy" Felsch set a White Sox home run record with 14 in 1920 and was having the best season of his six-year career, batting .338, when it all was terminated because of his participation in the "Black Sox" scandal. Felsch's lifetime batting average was .293, and his career was over at age 29.

Oscar "Happy" Felsch became the first Sox player to drive in more than 100 runs in a season (102 in 1917). He also was the first to hit more than 10 home runs in a season (14 in 1920).

Left: Two great leaders in major league baseball meet here, circa 1920: White Sox owner Charles A. Comiskey (left) and Cubs owner William Veeck. *(Photo courtesy of the Chicago Historical Society.)*

Below: Kicking off the season, 1920s style.

Eddie Collins played 12 productive years with the White Sox (1915-1926) between two stints with the Philadelphia A's. One of the game's greatest hitters (lifetime average, .333), Collins was also a brilliant fielder and one of the most successful base thieves in major league history. During his 25-year career in the majors, Collins played in 2,825 games, batted 9,949 times, got 3,310 hits and stole 743 bases. But despite hitting as high as .369 in a single season (1920), he never led the league in batting.

EDDIE COLLINS' CAREER WITH THE WHITE SOX

Year	Batting Average	2B	3B	HR	RBIs	Stolen Bases
1915	.332	22	10	4	77	46
1916	.308	14	17	0	52	40
1917	.289	18	12	0	67	53
1918*	.276	8	2	2	30	22
1919	.319	19	7	4	80	33
1920	.372	38	13	3	76	19
1921	.337	20	10	2	58	12
1922	.324	20	12	1	69	20
1923	.360	22	5	5	67	47
1924	.349	27	7	6	86	42
1925	.346	26	3	3	80	19
1926	.344	32	4	1	62	13
Career	**.330**	**266**	**101**	**31**	**804**	**366**

*In military service most of the season

Kid Gleason remained at the helm of the Sox after the scandal, all the way through the 1923 season. Johnny Mostil had replaced Shoeless Joe Jackson in the outfield, and would remain a stalwart there for the rest of the decade. It cost the Comiskeys $100,000 to fill the void at third base left by Buck Weaver, the hefty sum they paid to acquire Willie Kamm. Bibb Falk also got his chance to play the Sox outfield, and he would prove to be one of the club's best hitters during the remainder of the 1920s. Outfielder Harry Hooper, a 12-year veteran and future Hall of Famer had been brought over from the Boston Red Sox. But the premier acquisition came in 1923 when right-handed pitcher Ted Lyons, a senior at Baylor University in Texas, was signed. He

Above: Players did not come cheap back in the Roaring Twenties. This is what it cost to purchase the services of third baseman Willie Kamm from a minor league club in San Francisco.

Left: Hall of Famer Harry Hooper came to Chicago in 1921 after 12 noteworthy years with the Red Sox. He played in the White Sox outfield for five seasons, batting .328, .327 and .304 in three of them. He was enshrined at Cooperstown in 1971. (Photo courtesy of the *National Baseball Hall of Fame.*)

Above: Charlie Robertson's claim to White Sox fame is the fact that he is the club's only pitcher ever to hurl a perfect no-hit game. On that day in 1922, he beat the Tigers 2-0, but while pitching for the Sox from 1919 through 1925 he never posted a winning season.

Below: Bibb Falk was one of the best hitters for the White Sox during the 1920s. With season highs of .352 (1924), .345 (1926) and .327 (1927), he amassed a career average of .314. Falk roamed the Sox outfield from 1920 through 1928 and then spent his last three years in Cleveland.

Johnny Mostil was one of the White Sox's brightest stars during the 1920s. An outfielder of exceptional fielding skills, he also batted a career .301 and several times led the American League in stolen bases. His career highs include a batting average of .328 in 1926 and 43 base thefts in 1925.

Johnny Mostil became the first White Sox player ever to lead the American League in runs scored when he crossed the plate 135 times in 1925. Only Frank Thomas shares that honor (106 in 1994).

Below: One of the most steady pitchers during the 1920s was right-hander Ted Blankenship, here nursing a wounded little finger. Blankenship's best year was 1925 when he won 17 and lost eight, posting the lowest ERA of his career, 3.16.

would debut in 1923 but not really establish himself on the Sox pitching staff until 1925. But from that time on through the Roaring Twenties, the Stock Market crash, the Depression, and World War II, he would be the keystone of the Sox pitching corps.

In 1924, Kid Gleason retired and could not be coaxed back by Old Roman Comiskey. So the Sox looked to the North Side for a new manager, and found Frank Chance, the first-bagger of the famed Cub double-play combination of Tinker to Evers to Chance. He managed the Cubs from 1905 through 1912 before moving to the Yankees and the Red Sox in ensuing years. Chance took the job but never made it to the dugout because of poor health (he would in fact die before the season was over). The job was given over to his longtime infield partner Johnny Evers. But Evers lasted only a year as the Sox sunk to the AL cellar for the first time in the club's history. Their dismal record of 66-87 left them 25 1/2 games behind the pennant-winning Washington Senators. The only highlights of the year were Bibb Falk's batting average of .352 and Eddie Collins' theft of 42 bases (part of the team's total of 138 steals – both AL highs that year); Sloppy Thurston won 20 games while losing 14; and the fact that five Sox starters hit above .300 (besides Falk: Collins, .349; Harry Hooper, .328; Johnny Mostil, .325; Earl Sheely, .320).

Collins replaced Evers the next year as manager and the Sox moved up to fifth place in 1925. They also ended up in fifth the following year. After the 1926 season, however, Collins went back to the Philadelphia Athletics from whence he had come some 13 years earlier. Sox catcher Ray Schalk became the team mentor.

Schalk's team of 1927 remained just outside the first division. It was the year that Babe Ruth hit 60 home runs for the Yankees and his teammate Lou Gehrig belted out 47 – the same year the entire Sox team hit only 36 four-baggers. But Lyons won 22 games, the most in the AL that year, and he and another Sox hurler, Tommy Thomas, each pitched 308 innings, another league high. The following year manager Schalk was replaced at midseason by Lena Blackburne.

By 1930, the White Sox hired their seventh manager in eight years. Donie Bush was his name, and in his two-year regime the Sox would lose 92 and 97 games respectively, finishing in seventh place in 1930 and eighth in 1931. It was in 1930 that a 23-year-old shortstop who would go on to become a true Sox immortal, Luke Appling, made his debut and got eight hits in 26 at bats (.308). That was also the year in which Lyons posted his third season of more than 20 wins (22).

Shortly after the close of the 1931 baseball season, Charles Comiskey died. He had been instrumental in the successful building of the American League, and was one of the most profound figures in baseball during the 30 years he guided the White Sox. He would be enshrined in the Hall of Fame in 1939 along with Eddie Collins, together becoming the first Sox figures to be so honored. His son, Louis, replaced Old Roman Comiskey in the front office.

Left: Art Shires, who had dubbed for himself such nicknames as "The Great" and "What a Man," became just as well-known for the use of his fists as for his baseball skills. Shires on two occasions blackened the eyes of then Sox manager Lena Blackburne. He also went into the ring to box Chicago Bears center George Trafton, to whom he lost a three-round decision. With the Sox he batted .341, .312 and .258 in two-and-a-half seasons (1928-30).

Ted Lyons pitched his only no-hit game for the White Sox August 21, 1926. The victims of the 6-0 rout were the Boston Red Sox.

Right: J. Louis Comiskey, son of the Old Roman, took control of the White Sox in 1931. He headed the organization until his death in 1939.

**Before an exhibition game in 1931, two Chicago pitching greats posed together at
Comiskey Park: Red Faber of the Sox (left) and Charlie Root of the Cubs.**

Lew Fonseca came to manage the Sox in 1932 after playing with Cincinnati and Philadelphia in the National League and Cleveland in the American League. His three years at the Sox helm were losers, an overall record of 120-198 (.377), but Fonseca had had a fine career as a player. He had a lifetime batting average of .316 with a career high of .369 in 1929.

Ted Lyons pitched all 21 innings for the White Sox May 24, 1929, in a single game at Detroit. The Sox lost the extra-inning affair to the Tigers 6-5.

The nadir for the Sox, at least at that point in their history, came in 1932 when, under new manager Lew Fonseca, they lost 102 games (only one other time have the Sox dropped more games in a season – 1970 when they posted a record of 56-106). Surprisingly, the Sox of 1932 did not end up in last place. That ignominious distinction went to the Boston Red Sox, who managed to lose 111 games that year.

The impermanence of Sox managers stopped early the next season however, when Lou Comiskey named Jimmy Dykes to replace the suddenly retired Fonseca. Dykes would begin a reign that would last into the 1946 season, and his tenure would become the longest of any manager in White Sox history. Before the season, the Sox had obtained Dykes, along with future Hall of Famer Al Simmons and Mule Haas, from the Philadelphia A's. (Simmons, who had batted over .300 in every major league season since he was a rookie back in 1924, had twice led the league in batting, .381 and .390 in 1930 and 1931.)

Dykes would also benefit from the arrival of several other first-rate newcomers in 1934, pitchers Monty Stratton and Vern Kennedy, and first baseman Zeke Bonura. Simmons hit .344 for the Sox that year, Appling .303, and Bonura .302. Bonura also hit 27 home runs, the most at that point in White Sox history, almost doubling the previous club record of 14 shared by Happy Felsch and Al Simmons. But despite all that hitting, the Sox ended up in the cellar with a woeful record of 53-99, 47 games out of first place.

Dykes led the Sox up to fifth place the following year, and finally back into the first division in 1936. That year, Appling led the American League in batting, hitting a mighty .388. The Sox, in fact, had five .300 hitters in 1936 – besides Appling, outfielder Rip Radcliff (.335), Bonura (.330), second baseman Jackie Hayes (.312), and outfielder Mike Kreevich (.307). Kennedy won 21 games while losing only nine that year, and the Sox had a new catcher in Luke Sewell, a 15-year veteran of the major leagues whom they acquired from the Washington Senators.

Sad Sam Jones pitched out the last four years of his long Major League career with the White Sox (1932-35). He appeared in his first major league game in 1914; 22 years later he would boast 229 wins against 217 losses (.513). His career with the Sox was less distinguished, 36 wins, 46 losses (.439).

Left: Two of baseball's all-time greats got together here at Comiskey Park before the first All-Star game back in 1933, Al Simmons and Babe Ruth. Simmons joined the White Sox that year after nine years with the A's. In his three years with the Sox, Simmons batted .331, .344 and .267. His lifetime average is .334, and he had such career highs as .392 (1927), and 36 home runs, 165 RBIs and 152 runs scored (1930). Ruth incidentally hit a two-run homer to help the American League win that first All-Star game 4-2.

Right: Two Sox catchers of 1933: Frank Grube (left) and Charlie Berry.

Left: George "Mule" Haas takes a swing at spring training camp out in Pasadena, California, in 1933. Haas came to the Sox from Philadelphia that year along with Al Simmons and Jimmy Dykes. Haas would end his career five years later with a lifetime average of .292, although his best season with the Sox was a percentage point below that figure. *(Photo courtesy of* Wide World Photos*)*

Above: Henry "Zeke" Bonura truly was the first White Sox player to carry a big bat, although this one is somewhat exaggerated. A bona fide Sox slugger, Bonura hit 27 home runs his rookie year (1934) to set a new Sox record, one that would be tied but not broken until 1950.

Left: In his second year as Sox manager in 1935, Jimmy Dykes shakes hands and exchanges batting orders with Connie Mack, who was then in his 35th year as manager of the Philadelphia A's.

In 1936, Luke Appling put together the longest hitting streak in White Sox history, 27 games. The only other Sox batters to hit safely in 20 or more consecutive games are Guy Curtright, 26 in 1943; Chico Carrasquel, 24 in 1950; Minnie Minoso, 23 in 1955; Sam Mele, 22 in 1953; Roy Sievers, 21 in 1960; and Ken Berry, 20 in 1967. That year Luke Appling also became the first White Sox player ever to win the American League batting crown. His average of .388 in 1936 remains an all-time White Sox high.

Luke Appling is to the White Sox what DiMaggio was to the Yankees, Musial to the Cardinals, or Williams to the Red Sox. A Hall of Famer, inducted in 1964, he holds many Sox career batting records. From 1930 through 1950 Appling covered shortstop for the Sox. A fine fielder, astute base runner, solid hitter, and team leader, he boasted a .310 lifetime average while collecting 2,749 hits, 1,116 RBIs, 1,319 runs scored and 3,528 total bases.

Right: Luke Sewell had toiled with the Cleveland Indians for 12 years and the Washington Senators for two before joining the White Sox in 1935. One of the most reliable catchers in the league, he played for the Chicagoans for four years in the twilight of his career. His best year with the Sox was 1935 when he hit .285.

Sox hurler Bill Dietrich pitched a no-hit game June 1, 1937, defeating the St. Louis Browns 8-0.

Left: Monty Stratton suited up and hurled a pitch for the Sox before a benefit game for him at Comiskey Park in 1939. A front-line pitcher for the Sox, Stratton lost his leg as a result of a gun accident on a hunting trip the year before. The Cub player looking on is one of base-ball's all-time great pitchers, Dizzy Dean.

The Sox continued to add new names to their roster. Pitchers Thornton Lee and Johnny Rigney came in 1937. First baseman Joe Kuhel was added in 1938. Mike Tresh was brought up from the minors in 1938, and would take over the full-time catching duties with the departure of Sewell the following year. Louis Comiskey died in 1939, but the family, headed by his wife Grace Comiskey, maintained ownership of the club. That same year lights were added to Comiskey Park and the first night games in Chicago baseball history were played. Taffy Wright came to the Sox from the Washington Senators in 1940 and hit .337 his first year, second only to Appling's .348, and he would follow it up with seasons of .322 and .333 before going off to war. And rookie outfielder Dave Philley made a brief appearance in 1941 before being drafted.

World War II depleted the rosters of all major league teams. Before it ended, the Sox would send many of their best players and practically all the promising newcomers to wartime service, including Appling, Thurman Tucker, Don Kolloway and Bob Kennedy. All told, 28 members of the White Sox would serve in the military during the war.

The first night game played at Comiskey Park was August 14, 1939. The White Sox beat the St. Louis Browns 5-2.

Above: Two stalwarts on the White Sox roster in the late 1930s and early '40s were outfielder Mike Kreevich (left) and first baseman Joe Kuhel. Kreevich, in his six years as a Sox regular, batted over .300 three times and .297 on another occasion. Kuhel tied the Sox home run record of 27 in 1940, and twice scored more than 100 runs in his six-year stint in Chicago.

Right: Bob Elson began broadcasting the play-by-play action for the White Sox on radio back in 1932. His career was a distinguished one, lasting all the way into the 1972 season. Elson, a renowned gin rummy player and baseball authority, would come to be known as the "Commander," and he would be honored with a plaque in the Hall of Fame for his services to several generations of baseball fans.

At the All-Star game of 1939, the American League squad's oldest pitcher, Ted Lyons, 38, of the White Sox, poses with the youngest hurler, Bob Feller, 20, of the Indians.

TED LYONS' CAREER WITH THE WHITE SOX

Year	Won	Lost	ERA	SO's
1923	2	1	6.35	6
1924	12	11	4.87	52
1925	21	11	3.26	45
1926	18	16	3.01	51
1927	22	14	2.84	71
1928	15	14	3.98	60
1929	14	20	4.10	57
1930	22	15	3.78	69
1931	4	6	4.01	16
1932	10	15	3.28	58
1933	10	21	4.38	74
1934	11	13	4.87	53
1935	15	8	3.02	54
1936	10	13	5.14	48
1937	12	7	4.15	45
1938	9	11	3.70	54
1939	14	6	2.76	65
1940	12	8	3.24	72
1941	12	10	3.70	63
1942	14	6	2.10	50
1943-45	(Military Service)			
1946	1	4	2.32	10
Lifetime	**260**	**230**	**3.67**	**1,073**

Above: Comedian Joe E. Brown got the call to throw out the first ball on a chilly opening day at Comiskey Park in 1940. He is flanked here by Sox manager Jimmy Dykes and Cleveland Indian chieftain Ossie Vitt.

Below: The White Sox of 1941: Left to right: Top row – Myril Hoag, Joe Kuhel, Bob Kennedy, Luke Appling, Taft Wright, Don Kolloway, Ted Lyons, Jack Hallett, John Rigney, John Humphries, Bill Dietrich, Bill Knickerbocker. Middle Row – Sharkey, Julius Salthers, Tom Turner, Thornton Lee, Monty Stratton, Lee Ross, Dr. Schact, Ben Chapman, Stevens, George Dickey. Bottom Row – Mike Tresh, Ed Smith, Dario Lodigiani, Ruel, Jim Dykes, George Haas, Joe Haynes, Jimmy Webb, Mike Kreevich, Pete Appleton. In Front – Bat Boy Pete Parvan.

For most of the war years the Sox languished in the second division. Appling, just before going off to war, led the league in batting a second time when he hit .328 in 1943. The Sox added a few players during the war years, like veteran Tony Cuccinello and others whose names would later become well-known, such as Joe Haynes, Orval Grove, Eddie Lopat and Cass Michaels.

The national pastime weathered the war, and baseball's popularity did not diminish during those years of sacrifice. Many changes in the game were in the wind – black and Hispanic ballplayers were in the wings, television was being developed, and talk of league expansion was becoming common.

The White Sox anticipated some changes of their own. But they headed off an attempt by a young Bill Veeck to purchase the club's ownership. Grace Comiskey had no desire to let go of the team, not then anyway. The hope was that the team could be restored to the type of dynasty it had been building when the "Black Sox" scandal devastated it so brutally a quarter of a century earlier.

Greetings! Pitcher Johnny Rigney reads his draft notice in the locker room at Comiskey Park. Looking on with foreboding are first baseman Joe Kuhel (left), Dario Lodigiani, the Sox third baseman, and catcher George Dickey (far right).

Left: Mike Tresh was the man behind the plate for the White Sox most of the time from 1939 to 1948. He was respected as one of the finest fielding catchers of his time. His son, Tom Tresh, would play in the New York Yankee infield during the 1960s.

Below: In his first year with the White Sox, 1940, Taffy Wright batted .337. He followed it with seasons of .322 and .333, then departed for three years of military service in World War II. After the war, Wright played three more years for the Sox and ended his career with a lifetime batting average of .311.

Luke Appling smacked his 2,000th hit August 13, 1943, the same year he won his second American League batting crown with an average of .328. Appling ended his career seven years later with a total of 2,749 hits, the most in White Sox history.

Above: Orval Grove of Mineral, Kansas, came to the Sox in 1940. He was the club's premier pitcher during the war years and finally retired after the 1949 season. His best year was 1943, with a record of 15-9 (.625), and an ERA of 2.75.

Left: Thurman Tucker was a highly touted rookie when he joined the Sox in 1942. He played center field for them through 1947 (except 1945). His best year was 1946 when he hit .288; afterwards he played three years with the Cleveland Indians.

Above: Outfielder/third baseman Ralph Hodgin was a key member of the Sox during the war years and on through 1948. A superb fielder, he also sported a lifetime batting average of .285.

Right: Wally Moses spent the middle part of his career with the White Sox, coming aboard in 1942. He had spent seven years with the Philadelphia A's, and would leave in 1946 to play five more years with other clubs in the American League. Moses was a fine all-around player, but the areas in which he would shine varied from year to year. For example, in 1937, he hit 25 home runs and stole 9 bases, in 1943 he stole 56 bases and hit only 3 home runs. His best year batting was 1936 when he hit .345, and his top year with the Sox was 1945 when he batted .295.

Ted Lyons, the Sox' winningest pitcher of alltime, was honored here with a vintage car as his long career with the White Sox was coming to an end. Lyons, who won 260 games and lost 230 (.531) while in a Sox uniform (the only one he ever wore in the major leagues), played from 1923 to 1946, with three years off for service in World War II. He also managed the team from 1946 through 1948. Lyons was inducted into the Hall of Fame in 1955. His other career pitching stats: 594 games; 4,161 innings pitched; 1,073 strikeouts and 27 shutouts; and an ERA of 3.67.

2

The Road Back

With World War II over, major league rosters were suddenly glistening with stars. In the American League, the White Sox would face teams like the Boston Red Sox, illuminated by such figures as Ted Williams, Rudy York, Bobby Doerr, Johnny Pesky, Dom DiMaggio, Boo Ferriss, and Tex Hughson; the Tigers with the immortal Hank Greenberg as well as George Kell, Hoot Evers, Birdie Tebbetts, and pitchers like Hal Newhouser, Dizzy Trout, and Virgil "Fireball" Trucks; the Yankees with the great Joe DiMaggio, Scooter Rizzuto, Snuffy Stirnweiss, Joe Gordon, King Kong Keller, Aaron Robinson, Spud Chandler, Fireman Joe Page, and a rookie named Yogi Berra. Cleveland had Bob Feller, Bob Lemon, Allie Reynolds, Lou Boudreau, and Ken Keltner; in Senator uniforms were Mickey Vernon and a young Early Wynn; the Athletics had Sam Chapman, Hank Majeski and Elmer Valo; and the Browns counted Al Zarilla and Vern Stephens.

The National League had stars of equal magnitude, legendary names like Musial, Schoendienst, Marion, Slaughter, Stanky, Reese, Furillo, Hack, Cavaretta, Pafko, Spahn, Sain, Dark, Vander Meer, Blackwell, Kiner, and Mize.

Out at Comiskey Park for that first post-war season, the White Sox fielded a well-rounded team, but with the exception of Luke Appling, there were no names to rank with the luminaries that sparkled in other major league ballparks. They were, however, committed to rebuilding;

that was the word from the Comiskey-dominated front office. There *would* be some changes, and one came rather abruptly.

After the first 30 games of the 1946 season, Jimmy Dykes stepped down, a veteran of 12 years at the Sox helm. Ted Lyons, at 45 and still on the player roster, stepped up to replace him. Another great

Sox hurler, Red Faber, also came back aboard, signing on as a pitching coach. Under Lyons the Sox won 64 games and dropped 60 during the remainder of that season. Fifth place that year was an improvement over the two previous seasons, and the Sox had missed the first division by a mere two games. The fans obviously appreciated it because they came out in record numbers that year. All told, 983,403 passed through the turnstiles at Comiskey Park to break the previous attendance record of 833,492, which had stood since 1920 when loyal fans cheered the previous year's pennant winners – at least before that flag turned to tatters.

The remainder of the 1940s, however, was a period of disenchantment. The Sox, under Ted Lyons, dropped to sixth and then into the AL cellar before Lyons would be ousted in favor of Jack Onslow.

The cornerstone of the team in those years was, of course, Luke Appling. A few old-line greats made their way into

Above: Dave Philley arrived at Comiskey Park in 1941, took nine turns at bat and went off to war for four full years. He returned in 1946 and played into the 1951 season, then made his way through the Athletics, Indians, Orioles, back to the Sox in 1956-57, on to the Tigers, Phillies, San Francisco Giants, Orioles and Red Sox before hanging up his glove in 1962. Philley was at his best with the Sox in 1948 and 1949 when he hit .287 and .286. His career average is .270.

Right: Former star hurler, Ted Lyons, was the White Sox manager from 1946 through 1948. His career as a Sox pilot was less distinguished, however, than that as a pitcher. The Sox teams he led won only 185 games while losing 245 (.430) and never were able to get into the first division.

THE WHITE SOX
1947

Rudy York	1b
Don Kolloway	2b
Floyd Baker	3b
Luke Appling	ss
Bob Kennedy	lf
Dave Philley	cf
Taffy Wright	rf
Mike Tresh	c
Ed Lopat	p
Joe Haynes	p
Frank Papish	p
Orval Grove	p
Mgr. Ted Lyons	

Above: Don Kolloway played for the Sox seven years in the 1940s, mostly at second but sometimes at first or third. In 1942, he led the major leagues in doubles with 40. During his 12 years in the American League, Kolloway batted a career .271.

Left: Floyd "The Blotter" Baker held down third base for the Sox during most of the 1940s. He was respected as one of the finest fielders in the league during those years. His lifetime batting average was .251.

Larry Doby became the first black player to play in a major league game at Comiskey Park when he and the Cleveland Indians met the White Sox there July 5, 1947. (The Sox won 6-5 that day.) Later Doby would play for the Sox, serve on their coaching staff and manage the team for part of a season.

On June 8, 1947, the White Sox tied a major league record by playing in (and winning) the longest 1-0 game in baseball history. They beat the Washington Senators that day after 18 innings, tying the record which had originally been set back on May 15, 1918, by the same two teams.

White Sox uniforms, like Hall of Famer Red Ruffing, although at 43 his real pitching days were over after an illustrious 21-year-career (six with the Red Sox and 15 heading the Yankees' staff), and first baseman Rudy York who had put in 10 meritorious years with the Tigers and another two with the Red Sox. But they were in the twilight of their careers and they came and went with only a brief stay in Chicago. Some other well-known names around Comiskey Park also departed: Eddie Lopat to the Yankees, Taffy Wright to Philadelphia, and Joe Haynes and Frank Papish to Cleveland. And there were some new faces in Pat Seerey and pitchers Bill Wight and Randy Gumpert.

The most meaningful change for White Sox destinies, however, did not come on the team roster. It occurred in the front office when Chuck Comiskey replaced general manager Les O'Connor, who had held the job for the previous four years, with Frank C. Lane. As Chicago sportswriter Dave Condon once wrote, "(It) signaled the birth of a wonderful White Sox era . . . Almost from the day he set foot in the fading Baseball Palace of the World, Frantic Frankie kept the pot boiling. A man dedicated to clearing away old wood, the old ideas,

Hall of Famer Charles "Red" Ruffing would make a brief appearance in a White Sox uniform the last season of his 22-year career in the majors. The 43-year-old right-hander would pitch in nine games for the Sox in 1947, posting a record of only 3-5. Counting his more illustrious years with the Red Sox and the Yankees, Ruffing ended his playing days with 273 wins, 225 losses (.548) and a career ERA of 3.80.

Left: Bob Kennedy came up with the White Sox in 1939 and played through 1947, with three years off for military service. A third baseman initially, he would later move to the outfield, and eventually to the front office of the Chicago Cubs. As a ballplayer for the Sox, however, he was better appreciated as a fielder than as a hitter, his best year being 1947 when he hit .262.

Below: A postwar pitcher for the Sox, Frank Papish toiled for a faltering team at Comiskey Park from 1945 through 1948. His best year was 1947 (12-12).

Pat Seerey hit four home runs in a single game against the Philadelphia A's July 18, 1948, the only White Sox player ever to accomplish that feat. He struck out his first time at bat before blasting the four in a game which lasted 11 innings.

Above: Portly Pat Seerey played for the Sox in only 99 games in 1948 and 1949, but hit 18 home runs for them, four in a single game. The rest of his seven-year major league career was spent with the Cleveland Indians.

At the close of the 1949 season, Luke Appling established a major league record for most games played at shortstop, passing the 2,153 mark set by Rabbit Maranville (1912-1935). Appling's record would be increased the following year (to 2,218). Eventually it would be surpassed by another member of the White Sox, Luis Aparicio, who would play shortstop in 2,581 games.

This duo was the cornerstone of the White Sox infield in the late 1940s: Cass Michaels (left) covered second while Luke Appling handled shortstop. Michaels would play for the Sox from 1943 on into the 1950 season, then come back for a curtain-call appearance in 1954; the legendary Appling was there from 1930 through 1950. Michaels' best year was 1949 when he hit .308 for the Sox and drove in 83 runs.

Luke Appling set a new American League record for assists by a third baseman, a position he had moved to temporarily, when he registered 10 in a single game on June 20, 1948.

LUKE APPLING'S CAREER WITH THE WHITE SOX

Year	Batting Average	2B	3B	HR	RBIs	Stolen Bases
1930	.308	2	0	0	2	2
1931	.232	13	4	1	28	9
1932	.274	20	10	3	63	9
1933	.322	36	10	6	85	6
1934	.303	28	6	2	61	3
1935	.307	28	6	1	71	12
1936	.388	31	7	6	128	10
1937	.317	42	8	4	77	18
1938*	.303	14	0	0	44	1
1939	.314	16	6	0	56	16
1940	.348	27	13	0	79	3
1941	.314	26	8	1	57	12
1942	.262	26	4	3	53	17
1943	.328	33	2	3	80	27
1944	(Military service)					
1945**	.362	2	2	1	10	1
1946	.309	27	5	1	55	6
1947	.306	29	0	8	49	8
1948	.314	16	2	0	47	10
1949	.301	21	5	5	58	7
1950*	.234	3	4	0	13	2
Lifetime	**.310**	**440**	**102**	**45**	**1,116**	**179**

*Out most of the season with injured foot.
**In military service most of the season.

Left: Big things were expected of Randy Gumpert when he came to Chicago from the Yankees in 1948. But these were dismal years for the Sox as a team and less than inspiring for Gumpert as a pitcher. He won only 29 games in Chicago over four seasons and lost 42 (.408).

Below: Bill Wight joined the cellar-dwelling White Sox of 1948 but could only win nine games while losing 20. The next year he turned it around, however, and led the Sox staff with a record of 15-13 and an ERA of 3.31. He pitched a third season in Chicago (10-16) and then was traded to the Boston Red Sox.

On August 26, 1949, White Sox pitcher Bob Kuzava struck out six successive Red Sox batters to tie an American League record. The whiffers from Boston were: Vern Stephens, Bobby Doerr, Al Zarilla, Billy Goodman, Matt Batts and Ellis Kinder.

and old plumbing . . . and bringing in fresh faces." The hiring of Lane did precipitate a whirlwind of trades and changes, and of development and growth. In just a few years, his management resulted in what was to become known through baseballdom as the "Go-Go" Sox.

Lane would ride with Jack Onslow through the 1949 season, but it was clear as the Sox limped along in the second division that a change would be coming. It came early in 1950: Onslow was fired after 30 games, of which the Sox had won only eight and were deeply submerged in the AL cellar. He was replaced, on an interim basis, by Sox coach Red Corriden. The man who Lane had his eye on to run the show on the field, however, was a minor league manager named Paul Richards, and that is who would choreograph the Sox movements on the field in 1951.

Frank Lane was indeed a trader. If he had not been in baseball, surely he would have wheeled and dealed in the commodities market or on the stock exchange. The deals came like a hailstorm. The

Above: This youngster attended his first spring training in Pasadena in 1949. His name, Billy Pierce, would become one of the most familiar in all White Sox lore over the next 13 years. Pierce was the premier White Sox pitcher of the 1950s and set the team all-time standard for strikeouts with a total of 1,796. Over his entire 18-year career in the majors, Pierce would win 211 games and lose 169 (.555) with an ERA of 3.27. His best years with the Sox were 1956 (20-9) and 1957 (20-12).

Right: A whole new era was launched in 1949 with the hiring of Frank C. Lane as general manager. It would bring an age of wheeling and dealing, and a continuing line of new faces to appear beneath the traditional White Sox baseball caps. He would take the Sox from a moss-gathering team in the second division and turn them into a pennant contender in just a few short years. Under Lane, the Sox would come to be known as the "Go-Go" Sox.

Sox sold off catcher Mike Tresh, pitcher Orval Grove, and outfielder Steve Souchock, and traded away infielder Don Kolloway. Within three weeks in 1949, Lane acquired Chico Carrasquel for infielder Fred Hancock and pitcher Chuck Eisenmann, then picked up Nellie Fox for catcher Joe Tipton. The Sox also traded for or bought such veterans as Hank Majeski, Phil Masi and Gus Niarhos, and brought up from the minors slugger Gus Zernial and pitchers Ken Holcombe, Bob Cain and Luis Aloma. There were two more major trades in 1950 – one sending Cass Michaels, Bob Kuzava and John Ostrowski to the Senators for first baseman Eddie Robinson, infielder Al Kozar, and veteran pitcher Ray Scarborough. The other trade send Scarborough and Bill Wight to the Red Sox for pitchers Joe Dobson and Dick Littlefield and outfielder Al Zarilla. The line-up Paul Richards would hand to umpires in 1951 was totally different from the one Jack Onslow had in 1949.

Below: In a reverse of procedure, Chuck Comiskey, Jr., presented a symbolic key to Comiskey Park to Chicago mayor Martin Kennelly in the early 1950s. It would not be until 1959 that the key to the city would in turn be offered to the Sox. Then mayor Richard J. Daley would present it to the club for winning the American League pennant.

Left: Gus Zernial, sometimes known as "Ozark Ike," came to the Sox from the minors in 1949; the next year, his first as a regular, he promptly set a new club home run record by belting 29. He also batted .280 that year. The following year Zernial was traded to the Philadelphia A's. During his 11-year career in the majors, he would hit 237 home runs. His best season was 1953, when he clouted 42 for the A's.

Gus Zernial hit 29 home runs in 1950 to set a new White Sox record. The previous one of 27 homers in a season had been shared by Zeke Bonura (1934) and Joe Kuhel (1940). Zernial also hit three home runs in one game against the St. Louis Browns that year.

Left: Phil Masi had a fine 11-year career with the Boston Braves before joining the White Sox in 1950. He provided some crafty catching and steady hitting for several years until Sherm Lollar came along and Masi retired. In 1950 and 1951, Masi hit .279 and .271, a bit higher than his career average of .264.

Below: The White Sox outfield of 1950 (left to right): center fielder Jim Busby; left fielder Gus Zernial; and right fielder Dave Philley.

In Sox annals, it is generally accepted that 1951 was the year the White Sox formally became known as the "Go-Go" Sox, the nickname applied because of their collective speed on the basepaths and patented hustle in the field. But in truth, the "Go-Go" Sox were simply the culmination of a long heritage of racehorse baseball.

In fact, since the team's inception back in 1901, the Sox were known for the ingenuity and velocity they exhibited on the base lanes. That very first year of the American League the team stole 280 bases to lead the major leagues, and Sox first baseman Frank Isbell pilfered the most individually in the majors that year, 52. Year after year the team either headed the AL in that category or were in close contention for that slice of recognition. And there were many great base stealers in White Sox uniforms. After Isbell came Sam Mertes, a terror in the first decade of the AL. Eddie Collins followed and even today ranks high among all-time base thieves. After that, there was Johnny Mostil, and later Joe Kuhel, Mike Kreevich, Luke Appling and Wally Moses. And in three of the five postwar years leading up to the "Go-Go" Sox of 1951, Chicago had led the American League in stolen bases.

On May 1, 1951, Minnie Minoso debuted as the first black player ever to play for the White Sox. In his first at bat Minoso smashed a two-run homer that sailed into the distant center field bullpen off Yankee pitcher Vic Raschi.

The job of filling Luke Appling's famous cleats fell to a youngster from Venezuela by the name of Alfonso "Chico" Carrasquel. He quickly proved to be one of the finest fielding shortstops in the game. He played for the Sox from 1950 through 1955, and his best year at the plate was 1950 when he batted .282. Carrasquel spent 10 years in the majors and had a lifetime average of .258.

Chico Carrasquel set a major league fielding record in 1951 when he handled 297 consecutive chances without an error.

THE WHITE SOX
1951

Eddie Robinson	1b
Nellie Fox	2b
Bob Dillinger	3b
Chico Carrasquel	ss
Minnie Minoso	lf
Jim Busby	cf
Al Zarilla	rf
Phil Masi	c
Billy Pierce	p
Saul Rogovin	p
Ken Holcombe	p
Randy Gumpert	p
Mgr. Paul Richards	

Above: Hank Majeski was another of the seasoned veterans who passed through the Sox line-up during the 1950-51 seasons. A respected third baseman, he batted .309 for the Sox in 1950, second highest on the club that year. His lifetime batting average is .279.

Above: Manager Paul Richards (center) posed in the Sox dugout in 1951 (his first year at the Sox helm) with two of his moundsmen, Billy Pierce (left) and Randy Gumpert. The Sox would break into the first division (4th place) that year for the first time since 1943.

Below: Jim Busby, the speedy center fielder of the original "Go-Go" Sox of 1951, symbolized the kind of racehorse baseball the team would play through the decade. That first year he batted .283 and stole 26 bases, second only in the American League to Minnie Minoso's 31. The next year Busby would move on to the Senators.

For the first time in their history the White Sox drew more than one million people into Comiskey Park in 1951. The total attendance of 1,328,234 would remain an all-time high until the pennant-winning Sox of 1959 would draw 1,423,144. Also in 1951, the Sox drew their largest home crowd to date when 53,940 attended a night game June 8th against the Yankees.

Not all of Marilyn Monroe's baseball tutoring came from Joe DiMaggio. The White Sox contributed some, as illustrated here. Pitcher Joe Dobson impersonated a batting coach and outfielder Gus Zernial acted as catcher in this preseason photo from 1951.

Nevertheless, it was the Sox of 1951 who gained the moniker they would carry through the decade of the 1950s and into the World Series of 1959. It would prove to be a period of great excitement out at Comiskey Park, season after season of fierce contention, of high hopes, frustrations, cliff-hanging suspense, and nerve-warping disappointments.

The "Go-Go" Sox moved into the first division in 1951, the first time they had entered that vaulted domain since 1943. They trailed only the Yankees, Indians and Red Sox, three teams which would rank among the all-time great clubs in American League history. The Sox had been in first place the entire month of June, a feat that only the oldest of Sox fans could remember from days long past.

The White Sox of the '50s were not only speedsters, they also exhibited some raw power, a hitherto unknown quality. In 1950, the year Gus Zernial set a club record for home runs with 29, Eddie Robinson hit 20 and Dave Philley clouted 14. The team total of 93 four-baggers was 50 more than the preceding season and the most in White Sox history at that time.

In 1951, Zernial and Philley would be

Above: Saul Rogovin was traded to the Sox by the Detroit Tigers in 1951. That same year he produced 11 wins for the Sox and led the entire American League with an ERA of 2.78. During Rogovin's three years with the White Sox he won 32 games and lost 28 (.533).

Right: Al Zarilla was brought to Chicago in 1951 to add a little punch to the batting order. Zarilla had played for five years in St. Louis with the Browns and two with the Boston Red Sox. He batted .257 for the White Sox that year and contributed 10 homers, then was traded to the Browns the next year.

The greatest Sox second baseman since Eddie Collins was Jacob "Nellie" Fox, who came from the Philadelphia A's in 1950 and remained in Chicago through 1963. A consummate fielder, he holds the major league record for the highest career fielding average (.984). He also holds the major league record for most consecutive games played at second base (798). Fox seldom struck out, and was a true clutch player. Five times he led the league in at bats and four times in total hits. In his 19 years in the majors, including three with the Philadelphia A's and two with the Houston Astros, Fox played in 2,367 games, batted 9,232 times, hit safely 2,663 times, for a career batting average of .288. Six times he hit over .300.

Nellie Fox set a White Sox record when he struck out only 11 times in 147 games during the 1951 season.

Nellie Fox led the American League in hits during four different seasons – 1952 (192), 1954 (201, tied), 1957 (196) and 1958 (187). Only two other Sox players have ever led the league in hits, Minnie Minoso in 1960 (184) and Lance Johnson in 1995 (186).

NELLIE FOX'S CAREER WITH THE WHITE SOX

Year	Batting Average	2B	3B	HR	RBIs
1950	.247	12	7	0	30
1951	.313	32	12	4	55
1952	.296	25	10	0	39
1953	.285	31	8	3	72
1954	.319	24	8	2	47
1955	.311	28	7	6	59
1956	.296	20	10	4	52
1957	.317	27	8	6	61
1958	.300	21	6	0	49
1959	.306	34	6	2	70
1960	.289	24	10	2	59
1961	.251	11	5	2	51
1962	.267	27	7	2	54
1963	.260	19	0	2	42
Career	**.291**	**335**	**104**	**35**	**740**

Above: Before a Sox-Cubs exhibition game in 1951, managers Paul Richards (left) and Frankie Frisch posed for the cameras in front of the batting cage at Comiskey Park.

gone, traded to the Philadelphia A's in one of Frank Lane's sweeping deals that brought the Sox Orestes "Minnie" Minoso. Still, the power remained. Robinson slammed 29 home runs that year and Minoso, Zarilla, and outfielder Don Lenhardt, who Lane had purchased from the Browns, contributed 10 each. The team total was a respectable 86. Robinson also drove in 117 runs, the first time a Sox batter had topped 100 since Gerry Walker's 111 back in 1939.

The White Sox of 1951 also led the league in hits (1,453), triples (64), stolen bases (99), and team batting average (.270). Minoso batted .326, led the league in triples with 14, and in stolen bases with 31; Nellie Fox hit .313; Billie Pierce won 15 games and Saul Rogovin had the lowest ERA in the league (2.47). Rogovin had come to the Sox in the spring in a trade that sent Bob Cain to the Tigers. The other chief acquisition of the season was "Jungle" Jim Rivera from the Seattle farm club.

Lane's biggest deal, however, came after the season. He sent Joe DeMaestri, Gordon Goldsberry, Gus Niarhos, Dick Littlefield, and Rivera to the Browns for catcher Sherm Lollar, infielder Tommy Upton and

Above: The White Sox of 1951, the team that won the nickname "Go-Go" Sox: Left to right: Top row – Joe Dobson, Nellie Fox, Gus Niarhos, Phil Masi, Billy Pierce, Harry Dorish, Joe DeMaestri, Don Lenhardt, Hollis Sheely, Ross Grimsley, Jim Busby; Middle row – Ken Holcombe, Randy Gumpert, Howie Judson, Bob Boyd, Minnie Minoso, Ed Stewart, Luis Aloma, Saul Rogovin, Lou Kretlow, Elser (trainer); Bottom row – Eddie Robinson, Floyd Baker, Chico Carrasquel, Jim Adair (coach), Roger Cramer (coach), Paul Richards (manager), Ray Nerres (coach), Leon Harris (coach), Ray Coleman, Bob Dillinger, Al Zarilla.

pitcher Al Widmar.

The revolving door in the White Sox dugout remained in full swing in 1952. Jim Busby was among the first to go and the Senators sent the Sox Sam Mele for him. Rivera's contract was bought back from the Browns. But perhaps the best example of White Sox transiency was infielder Willie Miranda – on June 15th he was traded to the Browns; less than two weeks later the Sox purchased him back and four months later again traded him to the Browns.

Above: Harry Dorish who went by the nicknames of "Fritz" and "Chunky," was a mainstay in the Sox bullpen from 1951 into 1955. During that time, he was credited with 36 saves and compiled an overall record of 31 wins and 20 losses (.608).

Above: Outfielder Sam Mele was an established hitter when he came to the White Sox to hopefully enrich their poverty-stricken offense in 1952. He stayed through the next season, batting .248 and .274 in those two seasons, but his most memorable feat was the 22-game hitting streak he came up with in 1953.

Right: Luis Aloma handled a good portion of the White Sox bullpen duties from 1950 through 1953. A native of Havana, Cuba, he played only with the Sox and ended his career with 18 wins and three losses (.857), including 15 saves.

The Sox were a threat through much of 1952, and even held down second place at midseason. They couldn't, however, keep pace with a Yankee team that boasted Mickey Mantle, Yogi Berra, Hank Bauer, Scooter Rizzuto, Gil McDougald, Billy Martin, Allie Reynolds, Vic Raschi, Johnny Sain, and Eddie Lopat; and a Cleveland Indians roster which had three pitchers who would be 20-game winners that year – Early Wynn, Mike Garcia and Bob Lemon as well as hitters like Larry Doby, Al Rosen, Bobby Avila, Ray Boone and Luke Easter. The Sox finished third with a record of 81-73 (.526), identical to that of the year before. They led the league in fielding with a collective mark of .980. Fox was tops in the majors in fielding for a second baseman with an average of .985 and also led the league in hits (192) and at bats (648). Minoso was the league's most successful pirate on the basepaths with 22 thefts.

Bob Keegan joined the White Sox pitching staff in 1953, as did old vet Virgil Trucks, 34, who was acquired from the Browns. It seems the most significant trade of that year brought to Chicago the previous year's AL batting champ, first baseman Ferris Fain who had hit .327. He came from the A's in exchange for Eddie Robinson and Joe DeMaestri. It did not prove a lucrative trade, however, because Fain was hampered much of the season with a fractured finger and hit only .256 for the Sox with six home runs and 52 RBIs. Over in Philadelphia, however, Robinson would bang out 22 homers and drive in 102 runs.

In a surprise move, brawny Gus Zernial of the Philadelphia A's tried to steal second base, only to be tagged out by former teammate Chico Carrasquel. The throw was from Sox catcher Gus Niarhos.

Lefthander Jack Harshman set an all-time White Sox strikeout record July 25, 1954, when he fanned 16 Red Sox batters in a single game at Boston. The record still stands today. Twice Big Ed Walsh struck out 15 batters in a game, in 1908 and 1910, and Jim Scott got 15 once in 1913.

One of the great fielding cornerstones ever, Chico Carrasquel and Nellie Fox, who handled the activities around second base at Comiskey Park from 1950 through 1955.

The White Sox of 1953 posted their finest record since 1920 when they won 89 games, a .578 win percentage. Still, they wound up in third place, once again behind the Yankees and Indians in that order. "Fireball" Trucks showed that, despite his age, he was still combustible and won 20 games, losing only 10, and becoming the first 20-game winner for the Sox since Thornton Lee racked up 22 back in 1941.

Only 15 of the wins were for the Sox, however; the other five were posted while he was still a St. Louis Brown. Pierce won the most games for the Sox that year, a record of 18-12. Minoso, the team's only .300 hitter (.313), led the league in stolen bases again, this time with 25; Rivera was second with 22. Mele ran up the longest hitting streak in the league that year, 22 consecutive games.

In the early part of the 1954 season it looked like it might be the year that the White Sox would get it all together. They were in first place most of the time, but closely contested by the Indians and the Yankees. The Sox had brought Cass Michaels back from the A's with the intention of converting him from a second baseman to a third baseman. Later they acquired one of the game's foremost third sackers, George Kell, who had hit over .300 in each of the preceding eight seasons. They also added longtime Cub star Phil Cavarretta, who was 37 but still could hit.

Above: When he came to the White Sox in 1953, Virgil "Fireball" Trucks was 34 years old but on the way to the best season of his career – the only one in which he won 20 games. The fastballer, who had spent his first 11 major league years in Detroit, pitched three years for the Sox, turning in a composite record of 47-26 (.644). Over his 17-year big league career, Trucks would win 177 games and lose 135 (.567) and post an ERA of 3.39.

Right: Ferris Fain was brought into the White Sox fold to alleviate the hitting problems that plagued the team in 1953. He had led the American League in batting for the two previous seasons, batting .344 and .327 respectively. With the White Sox, however, he was hobbled by injuries during his two years in Chicago. He did bat .302 for the half-season he played in 1954, but was traded to Detroit the following year. Fain's lifetime batting average is .290.

Above: One of the game's rare slugging short-stops, Vern Stephens, made a transient appearance in a White Sox uniform in 1953. He played 44 games, but his heyday was over by that time. During Stephens' 15 years in the majors – spent mostly with the St. Louis Browns and Boston Red Sox – he clobbered 247 home runs (only one for the White Sox) and drove in 1,174 runs.

Below: A native Chicagoan, Johnny Groth played in his hometown in 1954 and part of 1955. Most of his 15-year career, however, was spent with the Tigers in Detroit. He batted .279 lifetime, and .275 the one full year he played for the Sox.

Left: Sandy Consuegra was 33 years old in 1954 when he posted a then record won-lost percentage by winning 16 games that year while losing only three (.842). Eight of those games were attributable to relief performance, another American League high that year. In the three years he hurled for the Sox, Consuegra won a total of 30 games and lost 15 (.667).

The fates, however, were not with Sox that year. Ace left-hander Billy Pierce was out an entire month with an arm injury. Fain banged up a knee and missed half the season. Kell played just a little more than a month before being sidelined for most of the rest of the season with a bad knee. And Cass Michaels was out in August from a fractured skull when he was beaned in Philadelphia.

As the season was winding down, Sox fans were jarred by an announcement on September 13th that manager Paul Richards had resigned. He was moving to the Baltimore Orioles where he would serve as both

MINNIE MINOSO'S CAREER WITH THE WHITE SOX

Year	Average	2B	3B	HR	RBIs	Stolen Bases
1952	.281	24	9	13	61	22
1953	.313	24	8	15	104	25
1954	.320	29	18	19	116	18
1955	.288	26	7	10	70	19
1956	.316	29	11	21	88	12
1957	.310	36	5	12	103	18
1960	.311	32	4	20	105	17
1961	.280	28	3	14	82	9
1964	.226	0	0	1	5	0
1976*	.125	0	0	0	0	0
1980**	.000	0	0	0	0	0
Career	**.302**	**228**	**65**	**125**	**734**	**140**

*53 years old, 8 At Bats, 1 hit
**57 years old, 2 At Bats

Orestes "Minnie" Minoso of Havana, Cuba, went to the plate for the first time for the White Sox in 1951 and the last, at 57 years old, in 1980. During his three tours of duty in Chicago (1952-57, 1960-61 and 1964) and his two late-in-life cameo appearances for Bill Veeck (1976 and 1980), Minnie always was the team rallying point. His great hustle in the outfield and on the basepaths (he led the league three times in thefts) were combined beautifully with steady hitting. During his 15-year career, Minoso compiled a lifetime average of .298 and stole 205 bases.

Left: George Kell was one of the game's finest hitters when he joined the Sox in 1954. For eight straight years he had hit above .300; his best, a league-leading .343 in 1949. In his one full year with the Sox, Kell batted .312. In his 15-year career in the American League he forged a lifetime average of .306.

Above: At 6'5", 220 pounds, Walt Dropo was a most imposing figure on the baseball diamond. The Sox traded for him to stock some power in their batting order in 1955, and he accommodated them by belting 19 home runs and driving in 79 runs his first year in Chicago. Dropo played two more years but neither were as productive as the first. With 13 years in the majors, Dropo could claim a lifetime batting average of .270 and a total of 152 home runs.

Left: Bob Keegan pitched for the Sox from 1953 through 1958. Sometimes known as "Smiley," he won 40 games and lost 36 during those six years. He also contributed one of the club's 15 no-hitters. His best year was 1954 when he recorded 16 wins against nine losses and had an ERA of 3.09.

Right: "Jungle" Jim Rivera held court in center field for the White Sox for most of the 1950s. Famous for his headfirst slides and great hustle, Rivera was one of the most exciting of the "Go-Go" Sox. His lifetime batting average was .256, his best effort being 1954 when he batted .286. He stole a total of 160 bases in his 10-year career; he was tops in the American League in 1955 when he stole 25 bases.

Below: Nicknamed "Scrap Iron," catcher Clint Courtney played 19 games in a White Sox uniform in 1955. But the rest of his 11-year career was spent with opposing teams in the American League. He had a career batting average of .268.

manager on the field and general manager in the front office. As he said in his letter of resignation, "I leave the White Sox with nothing but the kindest of feelings for club officials and players . . . Chuck Comiskey, through his mother, made me a fair offer. One I would not turn down without the opportunities a position of General Manager offers." The White Sox, of course, already had a general manager of exceptional note in Frank Lane. Moved up to manager was White Sox coach and the one-time great at shortstop for the St. Louis Cardinals, Marty Marion.

At season's end the Sox had posted their best record since 1920, winning 94 and losing 60 (.610). They were relegated to third place, however, with the only change in the year-end standings being that this time the Indians prevailed and the Yankees were reduced to runners-up. Again the "Go-Go" Sox led the majors in stolen bases (98), and the AL in team fielding (.982).

Among the outstanding individual performances was reliever Sandy Consuegra, posting the majors' top won-lost percentage. His .842 that year (16-3) was a club record. Fireball Trucks almost won 20 games for the Sox (19-12), and did pitch two one-hit shutouts that year. Minoso's 18 triples were by far the most in the majors, and he and Rivera stole the most bases for the Sox (18). Fox batted a career high of .319, and at one point had a 17-game hitting streak. He also stole 16 bases.

There was only one trade of note to precede the 1955 season. Fain was swapped to the Tigers for first baseman and slugger Walt Dropo. Another new face was right-hander Dick Donovan. And Marty Marion was given a vote of confidence with a new two-year contract as manager.

Donovan indeed appeared to be a lucrative find as he winged his way through the first half of the 1955 season, recording 13 wins and only four losses. But again the cruel fates frowned on the White Sox when Donovan was rushed to a hospital for the removal of his appendix. The Sox remained in the pennant race well into August, and the lead changed hands regularly between the Sox, the Yankees, and the Indians. As late as the first week in September the Sox were in first place, but then they faded. When it was all over, the Yankees had regained the AL pennant, three games ahead of the Indians and five over the White Sox. The Sox won 91 games that year and occupied first place for a total of 27 days and second place for 61 days.

Dick Donovan brought great hope to the White Sox pitching staff when he joined it in 1955. That first season he rattled off 15 wins against nine losses. His best year was 1957 (16-6), producing a league-high won-lost percentage of .727. In the six years Donovan pitched for the Sox (1955-60), he won 73 games and lost 50 (.593).

The Sox were still the league's masters of the basepaths, only in 1955 Rivera earned the individual crown with 25 while Minoso had to settle for 19. The White Sox also hit 116 home runs that year, the first time in the team's history that they ever exceeded the century mark. Walt Dropo was high with 19, Lollar had 16, Carrasquel and Bob Neiman had 11 each, and Rivera and Minoso, 10 apiece.

Frank Lane, who had brought so much flash and dazzle to the Sox in the first half of the 1950s announced at season's end that he was resigning to become general manager of the St. Louis Cardinals. Chuck Comiskey and John Rigney, who moved up to a vice president after Lane's departure, would run the team's day-to-day operations. Among their first acts was to trade Carrasquel and Jim Busby to the Indians for Larry Doby. At 31, Doby had hit .291 the season before and slugged 26 home runs. A week later, Trucks was dealt to the Tigers for outfielder/third baseman Bubba Phillips.

Above: Gerry Staley was a nine-year veteran when he showed up in Chicago in 1956. A starter most of his career, the Sox turned him into a first-class relief pitcher. He appeared in four of the 1959 World Series games for them and was credited with one save. During Staley's five years with the Sox, he registered 38 wins, 25 losses and 39 saves.

Right: A hometown boy, Sammy Esposito was a utility infielder for the White Sox from 1952 into 1963. He was also one of Chicago's all-time great high school football players.

Left: Before the 1956 season opener at Comiskey Park, Sox manager Marty Marion (left) shook hands with Cleveland Indians helmsman Al Lopez. The next year Lopez would change uniforms in order to guide the White Sox fortunes. (What the papier-mache Sox batter symbolized was never fully explained.)

Right: Luis Aparicio, from Maracaibo, Venezuela, broke in as a rookie with the Sox in 1956 and not only immediately won the starting job at short-stop but took Rookie of the Year honors as well. One of the finest fielding shortstops ever, he also was one of the game's great base thieves. Aparicio led the league in stolen bases nine con-secutive years (1956-64), the first seven of which were in a Sox uniform. Aparicio batted 10,230 times in his 18-year career and compiled a lifetime average of .262, while stealing a total of 506 bases.

The 1956 season proved to be depressingly similar to the four years that preceded it. The Sox were in the pennant race, then out of it, again combating the awesome Yankees and Indians. And for the fifth year running, they ended up holding the show ticket; the Yankees taking the win and the Indians the place. It was Billy Pierce's first 20-win season (20-9). Another pleasant note was the performance of rookie short-stop Luis Aparicio. He proved to be a miraculous fielder and stole 21 bases to lead the "Go-Go" Sox thieves that year. Larry Doby slammed out the most home runs (24) as the team set a new club record for four-baggers (128).

Before the year 1956 was out, Grace Comiskey died. She had served as the organization's president since 1941 and held the distinction of being the only woman to head a baseball club in American League history. The ownership after her death was divided between her daughter, Dorothy Rigney (54 percent) and son, Chuck Comiskey (46 percent).

Marty Marion's career as a White Sox manager came to an end with the close of the 1956 season. Chuck Comiskey and John Rigney looked to their all-too-recent rival, the Indians, for a replacement. Al "Señor" Lopez had guided the fortunes in Cleveland since 1951 and had brought the

Above: As a Red Sox hurler, Ellis Kinder had boondoggled the White Sox for years before he joined them in 1956. At one point he even won 17 straight against the Sox. He was at the end of his career when he donned a White Sox uniform but still won three games for them and lost one before retiring. Lifetime, he had 102 wins, 71 losses (.590).

Right: Pitcher Jack Harshman crosses home plate after bashing a three-run homer in this 1956 game against the Detroit Tigers. It was Harshman's best year in the majors: a pitching record of 15-11 (.577), and a total of six home runs to aid his various causes. Harshman actually hit 21 home runs in his eight-year major league career. Shaking hands with him here is Fred Hatfield (3) and looking on are Luis Aparicio (11) and Jim Rivera (7).

Indians to one pennant and five second-place finishes in those six years.

The White Sox picked up a new outfielder when they drafted fleet-footed Jim Landis. And before the season was long underway they acquired a new first baseman from the Tigers, Earl Torgeson, for Dave Philley.

The Señor was able to break the White Sox out of the third-place rut they had been in for the past five years. The team, in fact, held down first place through June but then faltered. They moved into second place that year after a volatile season, trailing Casey Stengel's mighty Yankees by eight games. Again the Sox were far and away the best base stealers in either league, toting up 109 in 1957. Aparicio nabbed 28 while Minoso and Rivera counted 18 apiece. Minoso's 36 doubles were the most in the AL and he drove in 103 runs, third-best in the league that year. Pierce again won 20 games, this time against 12 defeats, and Donovan's won-lost percentage of .727 (16-6) was tops in the majors.

Lopez was considered one of the game's great masterminds. Without him, the Indians skidded all the way down to sixth place in 1957. His stated goal was to bring a pennant to Chicago, a city which had not seen one, at least in the American League, since 1919. And that pennant year was a bitter memory. It looked as if he and the Sox management were going to pull out all the stops to accomplish that goal in 1958. There were some astonishing trades before the season. Minoso, one of the Sox fans' great favorites and an outstanding performer for the club during the past six seasons, was dealt to the Indians for ace pitcher Early Wynn (38 years old) and outfielder Al Smith. Larry Doby and pitcher Jack Harshman were also traded. They went to the Orioles in exchange for infielder Billy Goodman, outfielder Tito Francona and pitcher Ray Moore. Francona would not stay long, however, moving on to the Tigers in June for first baseman Ray Boone and pitcher Bob Shaw.

Despite all the talk of a pennant before the season, of how the Yankees were finally to be conquered – almost from the moment the first ball of the 1958 season was thrown – the White Sox foundered. In no way did they resemble the contenders they had been each year since 1952. They were quickly pounded into the second division; by June 15th, they were in the American League cellar. It would not be until August 9th before they could claim as many wins as they had

Earl Battey was a back-up catcher with the Sox from 1955 through 1959, playing behind Sherm Lollar. He would go on, however, to a fine career on his own with the Minnesota Twins from 1961 through 1967. In his major-league career, Battey would maintain a batting average of .270.

Righthander Bob Keegan pitched a no-hit game for the White Sox August 20, 1957, beating the Washington Senators 6-0. It was the first White Sox no-hitter in 20 years.

THE WHITE SOX
1957

Earl Torgeson	1b
Nellie Fox	2b
Bubba Phillips	3b
Luis Aparicio	ss
Minnie Minoso	lf
Jim Rivera	cf
Larry Doby	rf
Sherm Lollar	c
Billy Pierce	p
Dick Donovan	p
Bob Keegan	p
Jim Wilson	p
Mgr. Al Lopez	

losses, finally edging over the .500 mark.

The Sox were never in contention that year. They did, however, turn the season into a respectable one in late August and September, climbing all the way back to second place. But the Yankees breezed through to their ninth pennant in 10 years. The White Sox ended the season 10 games behind them with a final record of 82-72.

Only Nellie Fox managed to bat .300 that year and he did not hit one percentage point above it. He did belt out the most hits (187) in the league, however. Wynn had a disappointing season, winning only 14 games while dropping 16, although he struck out more batters (179) than anyone else in the league. Again Pierce led the Sox pitching staff, this time with a record of 17-11. And as usual the Sox led the majors in stolen bases (101); in fact, Luis Aparicio, Jim Rivera and Jim Landis, with 29, 21, and 19 thefts respectively, ranked one-two-three in that category in the AL.

The Señor was unhappy with the season, but not with the corps of talent he possessed. He said the Sox had the makings of a league champion, although they certainly hadn't played like it in 1958. The fans were more skeptical, and had shown their displeasure by staying away from the ballpark. Attendance at Comiskey Park was down to 797,451, the first time in seven years that the club had not drawn over a million, and over 335,000 less than the previous year.

But things were about to change. The Yankees would finally prove to be a team of mortal men, and Lopez, in regard to the formidability of the White Sox as a ball club, would prove prescient. The "Go-Go" Sox were about to treat the citizens of Chicago to one of the most exciting seasons in that town's long baseball history.

Earl Torgeson, without his trademark spectacles, takes batting practice. Torgy played first base for the Sox from 1957 into 1961 after nine years in the National League and two with the Tigers, Torgeson's lifetime batting average is .265; his best single season was with the Braves in 1950 when he hit .290, scored 120 runs (the league high), and hit 23 home runs.

Luis Aparicio successfully stole 26 consecutive bases in 1958. His string was finally broken when Yogi Berra threw him out June 2nd at Yankee Stadium.

At Comiskey Park, the "Go-Go" Sox displayed their Gold Glove awards, which had just been presented by officials of *The Sporting News* (left to right): left fielder Minnie Minoso; center fielder Jim Landis; shortstop Luis Aparicio and second baseman Nellie Fox.

On April 22, 1959, the White Sox performed a most amazing feat. They scored 11 runs in a single inning on just one hit. The deluge of runs came about as the result of 10 walks, a hit batsman and a lone hit in the seventh inning. The Sox annihilated the Kansas City A's 20-6 that day.

Sox owner Chuck Comiskey at Spring training in Tampa, Florida, in 1959 was not firing a bazooka at enemy players but instead was demonstrating the club's new automatic pitching machine. Looking on amusedly were pitchers (left to right) Dick Donovan, Early Wynn and Billy Pierce.

3
A Pennant, and After...

The year 1959 was to offer a variety of unique events in the United States. Alaska and Hawaii were admitted as the 49th and 50th states. The St. Lawrence Seaway was opened. Soviet premier Nikita Khrushchev toured the United States but was not allowed to visit Disneyland. The fabled New York Yankees fell from grace. And air raid sirens in Chicago shrieked out to awaken the entire city one September night, not to warn of impending doom but to herald the winner of baseball's coveted pennant.

The first sign that it was going to be an extraordinary year in the White Sox story came early. In February, a syndicate headed by Bill Veeck, Arthur Allyn and Hank Greenberg exercised the option which had been extended to them by Dorothy Rigney to buy her controlling block of stock in the White Sox. The following month the deal was consummated and the syndicate purchased her share of the ball club (54 percent) for a recorded $2.7 million. For the first time in its 58 years of existence the White Sox would not be controlled by the Comiskey family.

Chuck Comiskey stayed on and still held his 46 percent of the team. When Bill Veeck was installed as the club president, Comiskey was moved up to executive vice president. John Rigney resigned. Although the front office was in new hands, the team on the field was not. Al Lopez was given a strong vote of confidence by Veeck. The team, too, would be much the same as the 1958 squad, at least the one that took the field opening day. Once the season got underway, however, there was some wheeling and dealing for a few veterans. First came Harry "Suitcase" Simpson from Kansas City for Ray Boone. Then Larry Doby again joined the White Sox, purchased outright from the Tigers. And late in the season Ted Kluszewski arrived from the Pittsburgh Pirates in what would prove to be the year's most beneficial acquisition.

Above: Bob Shaw, in his first full year with the White Sox, 1959, chalked up 18 wins against six losses, and his won-lost percentage of .750 was the best in the American League. He also was credited with one win and a loss in that year's World Series. Shaw only pitched another year and a half in Chicago, and his record with the Sox was 38 wins and 25 losses (.603).

Right: Billy Goodman had a long and successful career as a utility infielder with the great Boston Red Sox teams of the late '40s and '50s before coming to the White Sox in 1958. He hit .300 during his 16-year career. Goodman's best year was 1950 when he batted .354 to lead all hitters in the major leagues. His best effort during four years with the White Sox (1958-61) was the first when he hit .299.

Owner Bill Veeck helped Manager Al Lopez celebrate his 51st birthday in the Sox dugout during a quieter moment in the hectic 1959 season.

The Sox started off strong in 1959. Lopez, along with Veeck, was talking pennant. The difference between 1959 and 1958, however, was that in the early going it actually seemed a realistic possibility. Through most of the season's first month, the Sox occupied first place. They were challenged most menacingly not by the Yankees, but by the Cleveland Indians, managed by Joe Gordon. In fact, on May 20th, the Yankees were buried in the American League cellar.

Through the All-Star break and on to the end of July, it would remain a hotly contested pennant race, with the Sox and the Indians exchanging the lead several times. But on July 28th, the Sox moved into first and would not move out again that season. Despite the fact that the Indians were not to regain the league lead, they still made a race of it which culminated the night of September 22nd. During the preceding seven weeks, the Indians had been as close to the Sox as a single game and as far back as six-and-a-half games.

The largest attendance at any regular season or World Series baseball game in major league history occurred October 6, 1959. It was the fifth game of the World Series between the White Sox and the Los Angeles Dodgers. The gate at the Coliseum in Los Angeles was 92,706. (The only larger crowd was at an exhibition game in the Coliseum between the Dodgers and the Yankees to honor Roy Campanella.)

September 22nd is historic in Sox annals because it was the night on which they clinched their first American League pennant since 1919. They were in Cleveland that evening to face the Indians before a crowd of more than 54,000. The Indians were in a do-or-die situation: a loss, and the season was virtually over for them.

Early Wynn – the premier Sox pitcher that year who had already won 20 games – took the mound. He got the lead in the third when Luis Aparicio slashed a double to right, scoring Bubba Phillips. Billy Goodman then followed suit with another double to right to send Aparicio across the plate. Jimmy Piersall, the Indians' center fielder,

Early Wynn pitched from 1939 all the way into the 1963 season, spending 1958 through 1962 with the White Sox. Five times he won 20 or more games – once with the White Sox, when he led the staff to the pennant in 1959. During his tenure with the Sox, Wynn won 64 games and lost 55 (.538). His major league career record is 300-244 with an ERA of 3.54 and 2,334 strikeouts during 4,564 innings pitched. Wynn was inducted into the Hall of Fame in 1972.

drove in a run for Cleveland, but Al Smith got it back for the Sox in the sixth inning with a home run. Moments later Jim Rivera followed with another. The Indians got another run and came into the bottom of the ninth inning trailing 4-2. Wynn had sat down in the seventh, relieved by Bob Shaw. And now in the ninth, Shaw was in trouble. The Indians had loaded the bases with only one out. Lopez went to his bullpen for reliable Gerry Staley, who pitched in 67 games that year. The workhorse Staley, however, would only have to throw one pitch that night. First baseman Vic Power swung at it and hit a hard grounder to Aparicio who grabbed it, raced to second for the force and fired to Kluszewski to complete the double play.

Staley was mobbed on the field, and broadcasters were shouting in the press booth. Back in Chicago hundreds of saloons filled with pandemonium. Their patrons, as well as those who watched or listened to the game at home, surged into the streets celebrating the news that Chicago had a winner, that the South Side drought was finally over. Someone authorized someone to turn on the city's air raid sirens to trumpet the victory, and hundred of thousands of other Chicagoans who had not been following the Sox-Indians game leaped from their beds thinking that the Russians had finally turned the cold water hot.

Word spread quickly that the Sox were on their way home and would indeed arrive in Chicago gloriously in the dark early morning hours of September 23rd. Soon, cars filled with fans were on their way out to Midway Airport to welcome home the conquering heroes. When the airplane landed, there was an estimated crowd of 50,000 people at the airport, including their most illustrious booster, Mayor Richard J. Daley.

When the final ball was pitched that season, the White Sox held first place by five games over the Indians and 15 over the hapless Yankees, who had somehow worked their way back up to third place. The Sox record of 94-60 (.610) had only been equaled once since 1920, in 1954. Fifty of those games had been decided by one run and the Sox won 35 of those decisions. When the gate was tallied for the year, the Sox had produced the biggest attendance figure to that date in their history. A total of 1,423,144 visited Comiskey Park in 1959, practically twice the number of fans as the year before.

Early Wynn, at 39, had a spectacular year, winning 22 games (the most in the AL) while losing only 10; his 256 innings pitched was also a league high. Bob Shaw won 18 games, losing six, and his percentage of .750 was the tops in the league. Pierce won another 14 games, while Turk Lown saved 15 (another league mark). Staley was second in the league, saving 14.

Aparicio led the majors with 56 stolen bases. Hitting had not been the Sox's strength that year. Fox was the only .300 hitter (.306) and the only qualified sluggers were Sherm Lollar with 22 homers, and Al Smith with 17. Lollar drove in the most runs with 84. The Sox had won it on speed, hustle, pitching and fielding.

In the National League, the crown was earned by a Dodger team that had defected to the West Coast the year before. A Cinderella team, they had soared from seventh place in 1958 to first in 1959. They were hardly a better-hitting team than the Sox (a club batting average of .257 to .250 for the Sox) but they had a lot of power in Brooklyn holdovers Duke Snider and Gil Hodges, as well as newcomers Charlie Neal, Don Demeter and Wally Moon. Pitching was their true forte – they had Don Drysdale, Johnny Podres, Roger Craig and a left-hander who was beginning to come into his own, Sandy Koufax. And they were managed by one of the game's all-time great pilots, Walt Alston.

The White Sox were hosts for the first two World Series games. And in the opener they dished up a real treat for the hometown fans. The once-weak Sox batting attack came alive, delivering two runs in the first inning, seven in the third, and two more in the fourth. The hero was Ted Kluszewski, the man of the famed bulging biceps, who slammed two home runs and drove in five runs. Meanwhile Early Wynn gave up not a single run. The final score was an 11-0 win for the Sox.

The next day it appeared the Sox might just be worthy of the 2-1 odds that bookmakers were now favoring them by – at least until the seventh inning. They had a 2-1 lead and Bob Shaw clearly appeared to be in command. He had given up a homer to Dodger second baseman Charlie Neal, but that was the only Dodger run that had crossed the plate. But then Chuck Essegian, pinch hitting for Johnny Podres, sent one into the stands to tie it. Junior Gilliam walked and then Charlie Neal whacked his second homer of the day. That was all for Shaw and all for the Sox as well. They added a run in the eighth but couldn't come up with one to tie it in the ninth. The 4-3 loss evened the Series.

Out in Los Angeles the next games were to be played in the Coliseum, a football stadium which had been oddly adapted to serve as a baseball park until the Dodgers could build a stadium in Chavez Ravine. The Coliseum could hold enormous crowds but some of the spectators complained that they might just as well have been in Pasadena since they sat so far away from the playing field. And the dimensions were incredible – 251 feet down the left-field foul line and 300 feet down the right-field line angling sharply to 440 feet in center. A 42-foot tall, wire-mesh screen stretched in front of the left-field stands to further deter home runs.

A record baseball crowd of 92,394 jammed the stadium in Los Angeles for the Series' third game. They watched their Dodgers shine. Behind Don Drysdale and Roger Craig and the flawless relief pitching of Larry Sherry, the Dodgers won two games in a row. But in the third game in Los Angeles the Sox came up with a 1-0 shutout through the combined efforts of Shaw, Pierce and Donovan, to bring the Series back to Chicago for the sixth game. In Comiskey Park, however, the Dodgers wrapped it up. Two runs in the third and six in the fourth broke the proverbial back of the Sox. The final score was 9-3.

The White Sox of 1959, winners of the club's first pennant since 1919. They would, however, lose the best-attended World Series up to that time to the Los Angeles Dodgers, four games to two.

Jim Landis races for the plate to score the second Sox run in the first game of the 1959 World Series, after tagging up on a long fly to center by Sherm Lollar. Hustling back to first base is Ted Kluszewski. That was the end of the scoring in the second but the Sox went on to add nine more runs and post a dazzling 11-0 shutout.

WORLD SERIES – 1959
Batting Order

Chicago White Sox

Luis Aparicio	ss
Nellie Fox	2b
Jim Landis	cf
Ted Kluszewski	1b
Sherm Lollar	c
Billy Goodman	3b
Al Smith	lf
Jim Rivera	cf

Los Angeles Dodgers

Junior Gilliam	3b
Charlie Neal	2b
Wally Moon	lf
Duke Snider	cf
Norm Larker	rf
Gil Hodges	1b
John Roseboro	c
Maury Wills	ss

The mighty Ted Kluszewski came to Chicago late in the 1959 regular season to pump some power into the Sox batting order as they made their run at the pennant. The Big Klu came through for them in the World Series when he whacked three home runs, drove in 10 of the team's 23 runs, and hit .391. He batted .293 for the Sox the next year but hit only five homers. For his 15 years in the majors, Kluszewski is credited with 279 home runs and a career average of .298.

WORLD SERIES – 1959

Game	R	H	E	Pitchers
Game 1				
Dodgers	0	8	3	Roger Craig, Chuck Churn, Clem Labine, Sandy Koufax, Johnny Klippstein
Sox	11	11	0	Early Wynn, Gerry Staley
Game 2				
Dodgers	4	9	1	Johnny Podres, Larry Sherry
Sox	3	8	0	Bob Shaw, Turk Lown
Game 3				
Sox	1	12	0	Dick Donovan, Gerry Staley
Dodgers	3	5	0	Don Drysdale, Larry Sherry
Game 4				
Sox	4	10	3	Early Wynn, Turk Lown, Billy Pierce, Gerry Staley
Dodgers	5	9	0	Roger Craig, Larry Sherry
Game 5				
Sox	1	5	0	Bob Shaw, Billy Pierce, Dick Donovan
Dodgers	0	9	0	Sandy Koufax, Stan Williams
Game 6				
Dodgers	9	13	0	Johnny Podres, Larry Sherry
Sox	3	6	1	Early Wynn, Dick Donovan, Turk Lown, Gerry Staley, Billy Pierce, Ray Moore

Early Wynn became the first White Sox pitcher to win the Cy Young Award, so honored in 1959, the year he helped the Sox to a pennant with a record of 22-10 (.688) and an ERA of 3.16. The 256 innings he pitched that year were the most in the American League. Only two other Sox hurlers have won Cy Young Award: LaMarr Hoyt in 1983 and Jack McDowell in 1993.

Nellie Fox became the first Chicago White Sox player ever to be named the American League's Most Valuable Player when he was so honored in 1959. Runner-up for the award that year was Sox shortstop Luis Aparicio.

Nellie Fox and Early Wynn seem happy here as they accept their honors – Most Valuable Player and the Cy Young Award – for 1959. The presenter is American League president Will Harridge.

Left: Outfielder Al Smith takes a mighty slice in what turned out to be his most successful year (1960) at the plate, batting .315, the club high. Smith came to the Sox from the Cleveland Indians in 1958 and played five full seasons in Chicago. His career average, put together over 12 seasons, is .272.

Right: Slugging Roy Sievers had been in the majors for 10 years before he came to Chicago. With the St. Louis Browns and the Washington Senators, he had earned a reputation as one of the game's steadiest power hitters. For the Sox, he hit 28 homers in 1960, one short of the club record then, and 27 the following year. In his 17-year career, Sievers hit 318 home runs and batted a lifetime .267; his 42 homers and 114 RBIs were league highs in 1957.

Below: Longtime Cleveland Indian ace Mike Garcia briefly wore a Sox uniform in 1960, but his career was basically over by that time. He appeared in 16 games, but recorded neither a win nor a loss. During his 14 years in the majors, "The Bear," as he was known, won 142 and lost 97 (.594), his best years being 1951 and 1952 when he won 20 and 22 games.

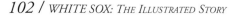

Kluszewski had an outstanding Series: three homers, 10 RBIs, and a .391 batting average. Fox hit .375 and Aparicio .308. It had been exciting. And it had been a record-setter. Thanks to the vast Coliseum, crowds of more than 92,000 had attended each of the three games there, enabling the 1959 World Series to become the best-attended Series in history, a record that would stand until 1970. A total of 420,784 attended the six World Series games and the players were rewarded with the largest postseason pay-offs ever, at least up to that time – each winning Dodger received $11,231 while each losing member of the White Sox took home $7,257.

The bookmakers and other assorted prognosticators were united in picking the White Sox to win the 1960 American League pennant. And the "Go-Go" Sox lived up to their pre-season notices with a fast start. The competition early in the season was not, once again, from the Yankees, nor was it from the Indians. This time it came from the Baltimore Orioles, managed by one-time Sox leader Paul Richards and inspired on the field by the play of Brooks Robinson. On the other hand, the Yankees were never out of the race as they had been early in the 1959 season. By August the Yankees' shadow grew ominous. It turned into a three-team pennant race. Then suddenly things were all too much like they had been in the '50s. The Sox faltered, so did the Orioles, and the Yankees surged behind the bats of Mantle,

Above: Sox catcher Sherm Lollar, about to put an end to the scoring threat of Baltimore Oriole base runner Gus Triandos, was the Sox catcher from 1952 through 1963. Acknowledged as one of the game's best during the late '40s and '50s, Lollar played 18 years worth of major league ball and ended with a lifetime batting average of .264. His best year with the Sox was 1956 when he hit a career high of .293, and twice he hit 20 or more home runs for the Sox.

Left: Sherm Lollar manages to deny the Washington Senators a run in this 1961 game. Coot Veal's foot missed the plate and Lollar quickly made the bare-handed tag. The umpire is Larry Napp. The throw had come from Sox second baseman Nellie Fox.

Herb Score was on the Sox roster the last three years of his career (1960-62), but he was never the same after being hit in the eye by a line drive in 1957. For the Sox, Score won only six games and lost 12.

Maris, Berra and Moose Skowron. The New Yorkers staged a dazzling stretch race, winning their last 15 games in a row to snatch the pennant.

The White Sox of 1960 had increased their batting power – the team average of .270 was 20 percentage points better than the pennant winners of 1959. Minoso had been reaquired, and hit .311, including 20 home runs and 105 RBIs. His 189 hits were the most in the American League. Roy Sievers took over first base as a result of a trade with the Washington Senators and he led the team in home runs with 28 – only one shy of the club record held jointly by Gus Zernial and Eddie Robinson – and batted an impressive .295. Topping the Sox batting order, however, was Al Smith, who hit a career high of .315 that year. Aparicio stole 51 bases, the most in either league. But pitching was weak, the best performance coming from veteran Billy Pierce (14-7).

The Sox ended up in third place, the first time a team managed by Al Lopez had finished below second in his 10 years of managing. The Orioles were second, two games ahead of the Sox.

The fans had been loyal. They came out in record numbers to Bill Veeck's new and improved Comiskey Park. The colorful owner introduced the exploding scoreboard to entertain Sox fans and rankle opposing pitchers when they served up home run balls. He had the drab old bricks of Comiskey Park painted white to give the stadium a fresh, clean look and had a picnic area built beneath the left-field grandstand. Those features and the presence of a reigning pennant holder were enough to attract 1,644,460 fans into Comiskey Park in 1960, a record season attendance figure.

The 1961 season was still in its infancy when the front office received a jarring blow. Bill Veeck, in ill health, sold his major interest in the White Sox to Arthur Allyn for a reported $2,940,000. The Veeck era which had promised so much was over after a scant two years – temporarily anyway.

The Sox continued their decline, dropping down to fourth place in 1961, trailing the Yankees, Tigers, and Orioles. They were never really in contention that year after an abominable start that landed them in the cellar by mid-June.

Left: Juan Pizarro came to the Sox in 1961 from Puerto Rico by way of the Milwaukee Braves. He would be a regular starter through 1966, experiencing his best year in 1964 when he won 19 and lost only nine (.679). He also had a fine year with the Sox in 1963, 16-8 (.667). In his 17 years in the majors, Pizarro won 131 and lost 105 (.556), threw 1,522 strikeouts, and could claim a career ERA of 3.43.

Below: J.C. Martin, who played occasionally at first and third for the Sox in 1961, crosses the plate after one of his five home runs that year. Martin would convert to catcher the next year.

Left: Dave DeBusschere would become far better known as a basketball player for the New York Knicks than he would as a pitcher for the Chicago White Sox. Nevertheless, he did wear the Sox stripes in 1962 and 1963, and won a total of three games while losing four.

One delight in an otherwise dismal season was the performance of young Floyd Robinson, who had been brought up from the minors late in the preceding season. He earned a starting berth in the outfield and led the club in hitting with a .310 average. Again, Aparicio was the majors' most successful base thief, this time with 53. Al Smith belted 28 home runs, and Roy Sievers hit 27.

With the end of that long season, several Sox mainstays departed. Rivera was the first to go, followed by Minoso, Sievers, Pierce and Billy Goodman.

The last vestige of the Comiskey family's association with the White Sox also vanished with the 1961 season when Chuck Comiskey sold his 46 percent holding in the organization. The purchasers were a group of businessmen headed by Tom Reynolds and Bill Bartholmay who paid an estimated $3.3 million for that block of stock.

Things got no better the next year. The Sox won 85 and lost 77, a percentage of .525, their lowest since 1950. When the 1962 season was over they had descended to fifth place. There had been little to cheer about.

On the plus side, Robinson again led Sox hitters with an average of .312, and his 45 doubles were the most in the American League that year. Aparicio stole 31 bases, another American League high, but was overshadowed by the record-breaking performance on National League basepaths by Los Angeles Dodger Maury Wills, who stole 104 bases, to demolish Ty Cobb's major league record of 96 set in 1915.

Speedster Jim Landis slides safely into second for one of his 19 stolen bases in 1962. Late with the tag is Baltimore Oriole second baseman Marv Bredding. Landis played in the Sox outfield from 1957 through 1964. During those years he stole 127 bases and was a key figure in the team's hard-running strategy. Over his 11 years in the majors, Landis compiled a career average of .247.

The Sox fortunes took a turn for the better in 1963. There were a lot of new names on the roster – pitcher Gary Peters, Pete Ward at third, Tommy McCraw at first, Ron Hansen at shortstop, Dave Nicholson in the outfield, J. C. Martin behind the plate, and 39-year-old Hoyt Wilhelm in the bullpen. It had cost the Sox to get those new faces, the most conspicuous losses being Luis Aparicio and Al Smith.

Floyd Robinson hit six consecutive singles in a game against the Boston Red Sox, July 22, 1962. He was six for six and the Sox won, 7-3.

Floyd Robinson hit 45 doubles in 1962 to set an all-time White Sox record, which would stand until Frank Thomas logged 46 in 1992.

Sox outfielder Floyd Robinson makes a spectacular catch to rob Chuck Hinton of the Washington Senators of an extra-base hit in this 1962 game at Comiskey Park. Robinson joined the Sox in 1960 and remained through the 1966 season. He hit over .300 three times during those years. Robinson's career average is .283, compiled over nine years.

The trend toward youthful players produced positive results, however. The Sox moved from sixth to second place, and suddenly there was some of the old spark out at Comiskey Park. Rookie southpaw Gary Peters led the league with a 2.33 ERA while turning in a nifty record of 19-8 (.704). Juan Pizarro won 16 games, and might have won 20 if he hadn't missed the last six weeks of the season with an injured arm. His 2.39 ERA was second only to Peters in the American League. Pete Ward, another rookie, led in the batting department with a .295 average, and slammed 22 homers, a club high for the season, which he shared with Dave Nicholson.

The 1963 team had been the most exciting group since the pennant-winning Sox of '59. It was enough to start talk of another flag for Chicago. But in 1964, the Yankees were still the team to beat, and they were as formidable as ever, having won the AL pennant every year since the Sox copped it five years earlier. In fact, the Yankees had topped the American League 13 of the previous 15 years.

Above: The youngster in this picture never played a game for the White Sox, but spent some time at spring training with them in 1962 and 1963. Just before the '63 season, the Detroit Tigers picked up Denny McLain on waivers. A native Chicagoan, McLain, of course, is remembered for his fabulous season of 1968 when he won 31 games, the first pitcher to break 30 since Dizzy Dean had back in 1934. McLain lost only six games that year for a won-lost percentage of .838.

Right: Dave Nicholson crosses home plate in this 1963 game after blasting a grand-slam homer against the Minnesota Twins. Floyd Robinson (3) had just crossed before him, and Jim Landis, Jim Lemon and Gary Peters were already queued up to congratulate him. Nicholson hit 22 home runs that year, enough to share the club honors with Pete Ward.

Right: Minnie Minoso always was one of the fans' favorites at Comiskey Park. It doesn't even matter that here, in 1963, he was wearing a Washington Senators uniform.

In 1963, Sox pitcher Ray Herbert hurled four shutouts in a row. For the season he racked up seven.

Right: Sox first baseman Tommy McCraw puts the tag to Los Angeles Angel Frank Kostro in this 1963 game at Comiskey Park. It neatly wrapped up an unassisted double play by McCraw who had just a second or two before speared a line drive from the bat of Jimmy Piersall. McCraw played for the Sox from 1963 through 1970. His lifetime batting average is .242.

Left: Gary Peters joined the Sox in 1959 but did not work into the regular rotation until 1963. That year, with a record of 19-8 (.704) and an ERA of 2.33, the best in the league, he was honored as the American League's Rookie of the Year. The next season he won 20 and lost only eight (.714), then in 1965 he led the league again with the lowest ERA, 1.98. Peters left the Sox after the 1969 season and played three more years with the Red Sox. His career totals: 124 wins, 103 losses (.546); an ERA of 3.25; 1,420 strikeouts and 2,081 innings pitched.

Below: The Yankees' fabled Mickey Mantle is tagged out by Sox third baseman Don Buford in this 1964 game. It was an attempted double steal.

With the accent strongly on youth, the Sox parted company with Lollar and Fox before the 1964 season. Lopez was not as confident about his youthful team of 1964 as he had been with the heroes of 1959, and his concerns proved to be warranted early in the season.

In June, because of a strangely devised schedule that year, the Sox had to face the Yankees nine times and the Orioles eight in a two-week period. The White Sox lost all nine to the Yankees as well as three to the Orioles and plummeted from first place to a full six games out. In midseason, however, the Sox managed a little explosion of their own with 18 wins in 23 games to make a real pennant race of it. In late August they even swept a four-game series with the Yankees at

Above: Shortstop Ron Hansen puts the tag on errant Red Sox base runner Bob Tillman after taking a pick-off throw from pitcher Gary Peters. Hansen took over the shortstop duties in Chicago in 1963 after Luis Aparicio was traded to the Orioles. He would hold down the post most of the time until Aparicio came back in 1968 to reclaim it.

Right: Pete Ward was an instant smash when he opened with the Sox in 1963. Edged out for Rookie of the Year honors by teammate Gary Peters, Ward hit .295 that year and drove in 84 runs – both team highs – and tied Dave Nicholson for home run honors with 22. The next year he blasted 23 homers and hit at a .282 clip, but from that point on his batting declined steadily. Ward played seven years in Chicago, and his lifetime batting average is .254.

Comiskey Park, the first time they had done that since 1956. By mid-September they were tied for the AL lead with the Orioles, but the Yankees loomed just behind them.

Then the Yankees – as they had so often in the past decade-and-a-half – turned it on, even staging an 11-game winning streak as the season came to a close. The White Sox won their last nine in a row, but it was not enough. They finished a game behind the Yanks. The Sox ended with a record of 98-64 (.605); those 98 wins were the second most in White Sox history after the 100 wins posted by the 1917 pennant-winning club.

Individual performances also were impressive. Gary Peters won 20 games against eight losses. Juan Pizzaro posted a record of 19-9, and Joel Horlen went 13-9 with an ERA of 1.88. Hoyt Wilhelm saved 27 games, registered 12 wins against nine losses and an ERA of 1.99. The pitching staff's overall ERA of 2.72 set an American League record that year. Floyd Robinson batted .301, and Pete Ward hit 23 home runs while Ron Hansen blasted another 20.

Everyone felt there was a lot of promise going into the 1965 season – young players who truly appeared to be coming into their own, a shrewd pilot, a lot of zest throughout the ranks, and substantial evidence that all might not be well in Yankee land.

The Sox started off in 1965 like veritable pennant winners; after a month's play they could glory in a record of 23-8, including a nine-

Don Buford, the Sox second baseman who sometimes played third, lines a hit to center as Kansas City A's catcher Billy Bryan watches it. It was Buford's best year (1965) with the Sox, batting .283 (the team high) and slugging 10 home runs. His 17 base thefts was also a Sox high that year but his finest year on the base paths would come in 1966 when he successfully swiped 51. Buford played five years with the Sox before being traded to the Orioles. His career average is .264.

Eddie Fisher pitched for the Sox from 1962 into the 1966 season and then came back for part of the 1973 season before retiring. His best year was 1965 when he won 15, lost seven, and saved 24 games; his appearance in 82 games that season was the most in the American League. Overall he won 46 games for the Sox and dropped 34 (.575).

game win streak and a berth on top of the league, and it was clear that the Yankee dynasty was indeed crumbling. But suddenly there was the Minnesota Twins to contend with, a team that had finished in seventh the year before, registering a paltry record of 79-83. In 1965 they were challenging the Sox at midseason and dominating them throughout the remainder of it. They won the pennant with a spectacular record of 102-60, seven games ahead of the second-place Sox.

Eddie Fisher and Tommy John headed the Sox regulars that year with records of 15-7 and 14-7. Hoyt Wilhelm posted the best ERA of his career (1.81) while saving 20 games. There were no .300 hitters – Don Buford was tops with .283 – but two newcomers to the Sox, first baseman Moose Skowron and catcher Johnny Romano, led the club in home runs with 18 apiece.

After the season, the Señor decided that at 57 he would opt for an early retirement. Lopez passed the managerial reins to Eddie Stanky, a fireball who had earned the nickname "The Brat" while playing second base in the National League in the '40s and '50s. He had most recently been serving in the front office of the New York Mets. Unfortunately for Stanky and the White Sox, their roller coaster was starting another descent.

Left: One of the ace fireman of all-time, knuckleballer Hoyt Wilhelm pitched 21 years in the major leagues (1952-72), six of them in Chicago (1963-1968). No one in the history of the majors has pitched in more games than the 1,070 Wilhelm appeared in. He ranks third in all-time saves, with a grand total of 227. For the Sox, Wilhelm produced 98 saves and an overall record of 41-33 (.554). He was elected to the Hall of Fame in 1985.

White Sox shortstop Ron Hansen set a major league record in 1966 when he successfully handled 28 chances in a doubleheader against the Red Sox. The White Sox won both games by identical scores of 3-2.

Right: Joel Horlen spent 11 years in a White Sox uniform and ended his career in Chicago after the 1971 season. His Sox record: .500, 113 wins and a like number of defeats. Horlen's finest year was 1967 when his ERA of 2.06, won-lost percentage of .731 and total of six shutouts all were American League highs. He won 19 games that year – including a no-hitter over Detroit at Comiskey Park – and lost just seven games.

A Sox publication referred to the team's problems as "a leaky defense and an anemic offense." Truisms, but there were also a bevy of injuries which benched Pete Ward, Ron Hansen, Gary Peters, J. C. Martin, and Hoyt Wilhelm for long stretches during the season. The result was a fourth-place finish in 1966 and their worst record in 16 years, 83-79 (.512). One of the season's few highlights was the performance of rookie outfielder Tommy Agee. He led the team in batting (.273), home runs (22), and RBIs (86). He successfully stole 44 bases, second on the club to Don Buford's 51.

After the season the Sox brought aboard a 25-year-old lefthander by the name of Wilbur Wood with the intention of putting him in the bullpen to augment the relief efforts of Bob Locker and the 43-year-old Wilhelm. They also signed Walt "No Neck" Williams and pinch-hitter Smokey Burgess; then, midway through the season, added veteran third baseman Ken Boyer and outfielder Rocky Colavito. And Luis Aparicio (age 35) was brought back from the Orioles to take over the duties at shortstop.

The longest night game in major league history involved the White Sox and the Senators in 1967. The 22-inning contest was played in Washington the night of June 12th and the early morning of June 13th. It lasted a full six hours and 38 minutes, and ended at 2:44 a.m. The Senators won it, 6-5.

Sox outfielder Tommy Agee proudly displayed the plaque he received from *The Sporting News* after being named the American League's Rookie of the Year in 1966. With him was famous Chicago sportscaster Jack Brickhouse. Agee batted .273 that year, hit 22 home runs, drove in 86 runs, and scored another 98, all club highs. He also stole 44 bases. It was by far the best of his three years with the White Sox.

Right: Beating out an infield hit for the Sox here is none other than catcher and famed pinch hitter Smokey Burgess. The rotund Burgess – never known for his base-running speed – played the last three seasons of his 18-year career in Chicago (1965-67). On retiring, he held two major league records – most at bats as a pinchhitter (507) and most hits as a pinch hitter (145). His career pinch-hitting average of .222 is, however, considerably less than his lifetime batting average of .295. The two Kansas City A's are pitcher Jim Dickson (with his foot on the base) and second baseman Dick Green.

Below: Bill "Moose" Skowron, who had had a memorable nine-year career with the Yankees, was in a White Sox uniform when in 1965 he joined the "200 Club," restricted to hitters who clout 200 home runs or more. The plaque was presented here by longtime Sox broadcaster Bob Elson. Skowron hit 28 of his career 211 home runs for the Sox. The most he ever hit in a single season was 28 in 1961.

AL LOPEZ'S CAREER AS SOX MANAGER				
Year	Standing	Won	Lost	Percentage
1957	2	90	64	.584
1958	2	82	72	.532
1959	1	94	60	.610
1960	3	87	67	.565
1961	4	86	76	.531
1962	5	85	77	.525
1963	2	94	68	.580
1964	2	98	64	.605
1965	2	95	67	.586
1968*	9	33	48	.407
1969**	4	9	9	.471
Career		**853**	**672**	**.559**

* Out of retirement to replace ousted manager Eddie Stanky
**Resigned due to ill health

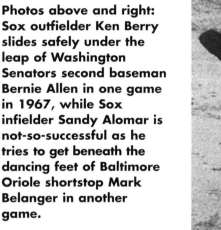

Right: Eddie Stanky, Sox manager, 1966-68. In the two-and-a-half years he guided the Sox, they won 206 games and lost 197 (.511).

Photos above and right: Sox outfielder Ken Berry slides safely under the leap of Washington Senators second baseman Bernie Allen in one game in 1967, while Sox infielder Sandy Alomar is not-so-successful as he tries to get beneath the dancing feet of Baltimore Oriole shortstop Mark Belanger in another game.

Still the Sox could climb no higher than fourth place in 1967, although they trailed the pennant-winning Boston Red Sox by a mere three games when the season ended (the Tigers and Twins had come in a game behind the Bostonians). It had been an exciting season, although another example of the "Hitless Wonders." The Sox occupied first place for a total of 89 days, and were in a tie for first at the end of the first week in September. Pitching was superb that year, with Horlen the club's premier hurler. He recorded 19 wins against seven defeats, and both his won-lost percentage of .731 and ERA of 2.06 were the highest in either league. Gary Peters won another 16 games and Bob Locker saved 20. But the team's batting average of .225 was the problem; it was the lowest a first-division team had posted since the White Sox tapped out a meek .221 in 1909.

Left: One of the game's premier home run hitters, Rocky Colavito brought his bat to Comiskey Park for a part of the 1967 season. He only contributed three roundtrippers for the White Sox, but hit a total of 374 in his 14-year career.

Below: Sox second baseman Wayne Causey takes a header here as Bobby Knoop of the California Angels tries to break up a double play in this 1967 game at Comiskey Park. Knoop succeeded. Looking on is shortstop Ron Hansen.

Left: Ken Boyer of the Sox dives for first base in this game against the Cleveland Indians. First baseman Tony Horton, with ball in hand, is not quite quick enough to put the tag on Boyer. The other Indian is pitcher Luis Tiant. Boyer only played for the Sox during parts of the 1967 and 1968 seasons. During his 15-year career, spent mostly with the St. Louis Cardinals, he compiled a lifetime average of .287, with a total of 282 home runs and 1,141 RBIs.

Right: A key member of the White Sox bullpen during the second half of the 1960s was Bob Locker. He contributed 58 saves to White Sox causes during those years, and in 1967 led the major leagues in appearances when he pitched in 77 games.

Sox catcher Duane Josephson illustrated how it is to be on both ends of the action at home plate during the 1968 season. Above, he puts the tag on an Oakland A, and in the photo on the right, he tries to slide under the tag of Detroit Tiger catcher Bill Freehan.

Everything changed drastically, however, and the bottom fell out for the Sox. Eddie Stanky did not last through the 1968 season as the Sox floundered in the second division. Lopez was brought out of retirement to replace the fired Stanky, but could effect little change. The Sox lost 95 games that year and won only 67. Their won-lost percentage of .414 and eighth-place finish combined to produce the worst season a Sox team had had since 1950.

The next year the Señor had good intentions of guiding the Sox back, but failing health caused him to bow out after only 17 games. Longtime Sox coach Don Gutteridge inherited the team. It was the first year of the new league arrangement which separated the 12 American League teams into two divisions. The Sox were placed in the AL West along with Minnesota, Oakland, California, Kansas City and Seattle.

For the White Sox, however, it was just the same as the year before. They slogged along and improved their record by a single game. At year's end the Sox had won 68 and lost 94 (.420), and were in fifth place in their six-team division. They had discovered some power in two relative newcomers, third baseman Bill Melton (23 homers, 87 RBIs) and outfielder Carlos May (18 home runs, 62

Above: The famous Johnny Sain never pitched for the Sox, but he did coach Sox pitchers in the 1960s.

Right: Tommy John was a regular in the Sox rotation from 1965 through 1971, and led the league in shutouts twice during that time (1966 with five and 1967, six). John's overall record with the Sox was 82 wins and 80 losses (.506).

Little Luis Aparicio was friends with everyone. Here he smiles along with baseball commissioner Bowie Kuhn.

RBIs). And they found an iron man in Wilbur Wood, who toiled on the mound in 76 games – the most in the American League that year, although his record of 10-11 was not a lot to get excited about. Walt Williams was the only .300 hitter; his average of .304 was the highest achieved by a White Sox batter since Floyd Robinson hit .310 eight years earlier.

Ownership of the Sox changed hands that year when Arthur Allyn, who by that time was sole owner of the organization, sold all his stock to his brother, John Allyn. In 1969 home attendance had dropped to 589,546, the lowest figure since the destitute days of World War II. And if that was bad, it was about to get even worse.

The year 1970 ushered out the turmoil of the '60s in the United States and there was hope of excitement in the new decade just beginning. For the Sox, however, it held in store something altogether different and despairing – the worst season in the team's 70-year history was about to take place, one that still remains as the club's all-time nadir.

Don Gutteridge did not quite last until Labor Day when he turned the team over to interim manager Bill Adair, who headed the club for

LUIS APARICIO'S RECORD AS A SOX BASE THIEF	
Year	**Stolen Bases**
1956	21
1957	28
1958	29
1959	56
1960	51
1961	53
1962	31
1968	17
1969	24
1970	8
Career	**318**

Aparicio led the American League in stolen bases nine times.

a week until Chuck Tanner, the new manager-designate, could finish up his business with the Hawaii team he was managing in the Pacific Coast League. The White Sox were in last place with a 49-89 record when Gutteridge departed. From there the team descended to 56-106 (.346). When the curtain mercifully came down on the 1970 season, the White Sox had lost the most games ever in a single season, and turned in the third lowest won-lost percentage in club history. They were in last place, 42 games behind the division champion Minnesota Twins.

Aparicio managed to hit a career-high .313, and Melton set a new Sox home run record with 33 during that otherwise forgettable year. There was nothing else in which to take pride. Less than 500,000 fans passed through the Comiskey Park turnstiles that year, the least since 1942.

As a result there was a major shake-up in the front office. Ed Short, vice president and director of player personnel, was replaced with Roland Hemond, who had been farm director of the California Angels. The new partnership of Hemond and Tanner geared up to make some changes, and alter the course of the Sox. What they had going for them after that awful season of 1970 was the fact that they had nowhere to go but up!

Walt "No Neck" Williams had six good years with the Sox (1967-72). Always a hustler, he had his best year at the plate in 1969 when he batted .304.

THE WHITE SOX
1970

Gail Hopkins	1b
Bobby Knoop	2b
Bill Melton	3b
Luis Aparicio	ss
Walt Williams	lf
Ken Berry	cf
Carlos May	rf
Ed Herrmann	c
Tommy John	p
Gerry Janeski	p
Wilbur Wood	p
Joel Horlen	p
Mgrs. Don Gutteridge	
Bill Adair	
Chuck Tanner	

Bill Melton hit 33 home runs in 1970 to set a new White Sox record. The previous one of 29 had been held jointly by Gus Zernial and Eddie Robinson. He also set another Sox record by hitting 23 of them in Comiskey Park; the most any previous White Sox player had hit at home in one season were the 21 Zeke Bonura belted in 1934.

In 1971, Melton would again hit 33 home runs and become the first White Sox player in history to win the American League home run crown.

Second baseman Bobby Knoop, who played for the White Sox in 1969 and 1970, was a Gold Glove Winner. He accepted the award from White Sox Vice President, Stu Holcomb. With the microphone was pitcher-turned-broadcaster, the former Red Sox ace, Mel Parnell.

The photo above shows the swing that gave Bill Melton the American League home run crown of 1971, the first time a Sox hitter ever won it. The photo at right depicts the congratulatory aftermath. Pat Kelly is slapping hands with Melton. Clouted at Comiskey Park against the Milwaukee Brewers September 30th, it was his 33rd home run of the year, the same number he had clubbed the year before. In Melton's eight years with the Sox, he hit 154 homers.

4

Allyn to Veeck to Reinsdorf & Einhorn

Opening day at Comiskey Park, 1971, was a surprise to everyone. The fans who had stayed away in droves the year before while the White Sox registered their worst season ever came out en masse to kick off the new season. A record opening day crowd of 43,253 gathered at Comiskey Park to watch what was labeled as the "new" Sox under their new manager, Chuck Tanner. And they were rewarded – at least that afternoon – as the Sox picked apart the Minnesota Twins, 3-2.

The Sox team on the field was indeed new. There were four new-comers in the Sox line-up – Mike Andrews at second, shortstop Luis Alvarado, and outfielders Jay Johnstone and Rick Reichardt. Carlos May had been moved from the outfield to first base. Wilbur Wood was going to be given a try as a starting pitcher instead of the reliever he had been his four previous years with the Sox. And youngsters Tom Bradley, 24, and Bart Johnson, 21, both right-handers, also would be new to regular pitching rotation.

Despite their success on opening day, the White Sox had a difficult go of it early in the season. But in the last two-thirds of the season they managed to win 58 of 108 games, enough to land them in third place in the AL West, a considerable improvement over their cellar finish the year before. The team could boast that they had won 23 more games in 1971 than they had in 1970. Still, they were under .500, although they had raised their won-lost percentage above the year before by 182 percentage points. In addition, they had enticed 335,000 more fans into the seats at Comiskey Park than they had in 1970.

What the fans primarily came out to see was the power-hitting of Bill Melton, who tied his own Sox record of 33 home runs in a season. Other Sox sluggers belted out homers that year, too – among them, Reichardt (19), Johnstone (16), Andrews (12), and Ed Herrmann (11); all told, the team produced 138 roundtrippers to tie the Sox record set in 1961. The other season highlight was the performance of Wood as

Above: Wilbur Wood – iron man, knuckle-baller, ever-reliable – stepped from the bullpen to the starting rotation for the Sox in 1971. For four straight years he won 20 or more games, a Sox pitching record. Until 1978, he remained the core around which the Sox pitching staff was built. Wood would bring the kind of strength and endurance to the Sox pitching of the 1970s that Big Ed Walsh had given them in the early 1900s.

Left: Jay Johnstone, taking a healthy cut here, played in the Sox outfield in 1971 and 1972. In '71 he hit .260 and stole 10 bases.

a regular starter; he won 22, lost 13, and turned in an ERA of 1.91.

Before the next season could get underway, the Sox made two major acquisitions. Slugging first baseman Dick Allen was brought over from Los Angeles for Sox pitcher Tommy John, and the Yankees sent pitcher Stan Bahnsen to the Sox for infielder Rich McKinney. The players would contribute substantially to what was to become the best White Sox season since the mid-1960s.

The Sox in 1972 would battle Oakland for the division title all the way into the season's final month. The A's, were extraordinarily strong that year. They had a pitching staff which included Catfish Hunter, Ken Holtzman, Blue Moon Odom and Rollie Fingers; hitters like Reggie Jackson, Joe Rudi and Sal Bando; and a shortstop speedster named Bert Campaneris. They would go on to win the AL pennant and the World Series that year. But the Sox made them work for it. And when the regular season was over, the Sox were in second place, only five-and-a-half games behind the A's. Their record of 87-67 was the first winning season for the Sox since 1967.

Below: Chuck Tanner held the Sox reins from late in the 1970 season through 1975. His first two full years were the most productive, bringing the Sox in at third and second place. When he left to manage the Oakland A's in 1976, Tanner had Sox career totals of 401 wins and 414 losses (.492).

Above: Roland Hemond came to the White Sox in 1970 when club owner John Allyn appointed him as a vice president and director of player personnel to replace ousted Ed Short. Hemond who was the farm club director for the California Angels before joining the White Sox, served under three different ownerships.

There were some exceptionally worthy performances that year. Wood won the most games in the American League, 24, and started more games than any pitcher in either league, 49, the latter figure tying the Sox record that Big Ed Walsh established all the way back in 1908. Bahnsen won 21 and lost only 16. It was the first time the White Sox had two 20-game winners in the same season since 1920 when they had four (Red Faber, Lefty Williams, Dickie Kerr, and Ed Cicotte). And 20-year-old Terry Forster saved 29 games for the White Sox, a new club high which displaced the record 27 saves racked up by Hoyt Wilhelm in 1964.

On offense, Dick Allen set a new Sox home run record with 37, and also led the league in that category. He drove in 113 runs, another league high that year. It was the first time a Sox hitter produced more than 100 RBIs since Floyd Robinson's 109 in 1962. Allen batted .308 and his slugging average of .603 was the American League's highest. May batted .308 and hit 12 home runs.

The honors flowed for the Sox that year. Dick Allen was named MVP in the American League, Chuck Tanner was cited as Manager of the Year, and Roland Hemond was *The Sporting News* Major League Executive of the Year. On the economic end, the Sox drew more than a million fans at home, the first time since 1966.

The White Sox of 1972. Left to right: Front row – Jim Riley, Rory Clark and Joe White (bat boys); Second row – Carlos May, Luis Alvarado, Bart Johnson, Al Monchak (coach), Joe Lonnett (coach), Chuck Tanner (manager), Johnny Sain (coach), Jim Mahoney (coach), Jorge Orta, Walt Williams and Jim Qualls; Third row – Charlie Saad (trainer), Larry Licklider (equipment manager), Glen Rosenbaum (batting practice pitcher), Wilbur Wood, Chuck Brinkman, Jim Geddes, Dave Lemonds, Rick Reichardt, Pat Kelly, Mike Andrews, Dick Allen, Don Unferth (traveling secretary and statistician) and Mike Morris (visiting clubhouse custodian); Back row – Ed Herrmann, Bill Melton, Rich Gossage, Terry Forster, Tom Egan, Rich Morales, Jay Johnstone, Tom Bradley, Vicente Romo, Steve Kealy and Stan Bahnsen.

Above: Dick Allen brought some excitement to town when he showed up to play for the Sox in 1972. A gifted athlete, but often a malcontent ballplayer, he would quit the team before the 1974 season was over. During those three seasons, however, Allen provided some sparkling baseball playing for Sox fans. The first year alone he set a new club home run record of 37, also the league high. He led the league in RBIs (113) and slugging (.603), and was named the American League MVP.

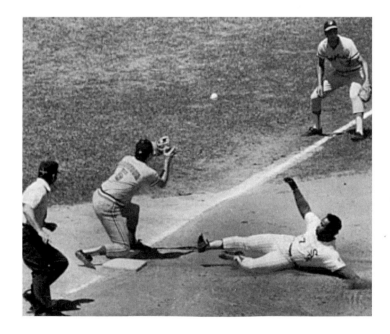

Left: Carlos May slides to beat a throw to Baltimore Orioles famed third baseman Brooks Robinson. Looking on is Oriole shortstop Mark Belanger. May was a regular in the Sox out-field from 1969 through 1975. His best year was 1972 when he hit .308, tying Dick Allen for the club crown. He also whacked 12 home runs and stole 23 bases that year.

The next year looked as if it were going to be even better. The Sox surged to the front early and were the predominant force in the AL West through the first two months of the 1973 season. But then the Sox world began to crumble. Severe injuries benched Allen and center fielder Ken Henderson for much of the season, and a spate of other minor ailments helped to hobble the Sox. They faded decisively. From a berth at the top of the division, the Sox skidded all the way to fifth place by season's end, 17 games out of first.

Wood and Bahnsen again combined to produce 20-game seasons, only this time they were posted in the loss column. Wood won 24 games, but lost 20, and Bahnsen lost 21 while winning 18. It was the first and only time in White Sox history that the team had two 20-game losers in the same season.

Above: Stan Bahnsen came up with the best performance of his career in 1972, the first year he pitched for the Sox. He won 21 games that year, losing only 16 (.568). The following year, however, he lost 21. His overall record with the Sox was 55-58 (.487).

Left: Sox catcher Ed Herrmann blocks the plate and it appears as if Oakland's Bert Campaneris is about to leap into his lap. Herrmann was the Sox backstop off and on from 1969 through 1974.

Late that season the Sox made one important acquisition, left-handed veteran Jim Kaat from the staff of the Minnesota Twins. At 34, Kaat had been in the big leagues for 14 years. His best year had been 1966 when he led the league with 25 wins for Minnesota. He had won at least 10 games every year since 1962. During the twilight of the 1973 season he won four games for the Sox while losing only one. But he would make his value better known in 1974 by winning 21 games to pace the Sox pitching staff.

Kaat actually was the only noticeable change in the line-up for the Sox that year. And there was not much change in the team's performance either, although it was somewhat reversed – this time it was a slow start with a gradual climb back up. But they could climb no higher than fourth with a final record of 80-80.

Above: The White Sox picked up Steve Stone in 1973 from the San Francisco Giants, then, after a 6-11 year, sent him to the Cubs for three seasons, only to retrieve him in 1977. That year he headed the Sox staff with a record of 15-12. Stone was traded to the Orioles in 1979 and in 1980 won 25 games for them against seven losses (.781), and earned the Cy Young Award.

Left: Center fielder Ken Henderson had played for the San Francisco Giants for eight years before coming to the White Sox in 1973. He would secure a starting job the next year and hold it through 1975 before moving on. In 1974, Henderson hit .292 for the Sox, and belted 20 home runs, second only to Dick Allen's 32 that year.

Left: Jorge Orta relays to first over the head of Oakland's Gene Tenace. Orta, a dependable fielder at second base, was one of the steadiest and most productive hitters during his Sox career from 1972 through 1979. Twice he batted over .300 (his best, .316 in 1974) and was always in the high .200s. He belted 79 home runs for the Sox.

Jorge Orta banged out five hits in a game on three separate occasions in 1974. It stands second in major league record books to the five hits made in four separate games in the same year by Stan Musial, Ty Cobb and Wee Willie Keeler.

WILBUR WOOD'S CAREER WITH THE WHITE SOX

Year	Won	Lost	ERA	SOs
1967*	4	2	2.45	47
1968*	13	12	1.87	74
1969*	10	11	3.01	73
1970	9	13	2.80	85
1971	22	13	1.91	210
1972	24	17	2.51	193
1973	24	20	3.46	199
1974	20	19	3.60	169
1975	16	20	4.11	140
1976**	4	3	2.25	31
1977**	7	8	4.98	42
1978	10	10	5.20	69
Career	**163**	**148**	**3.18**	**1,332**

*Principally served as a relief pitcher.
**Out most of the season with an injured knee.

Above: Wilbur Wood could also be a demon on the base paths, illustrated here as he slides in to score.

The most startling event of the season, however, occurred in September. Dick Allen, the ever-volatile and never-predictable Sox first baseman announced his retirement. At the time, he was leading the league in home runs (32) and had the top slugging average (.563). When the season ended two weeks later those figures were still the league's best. He also was batting .301. After the season, team management placed Allen on the "disqualified" list because he had never sent them a formal letter of retirement. But whatever his status, the White Sox's biggest star of the '70s was suddenly extinguished, at least in Chicago.

Jim Kaat posted a 21-13 record in 1974. Wilbur Wood had 20 games to his credit for the fourth consecutive season (20-19) and Terry Forster led the league with 24 saves. Jorge Orta hit .316 and Ken Henderson .292. The Sox led the entire American League in home runs that year with 135. Besides Allen's 32, Bill Melton cracked 21, Henderson, 20, and Orta, Ed Herrmann, and Brian Downing had 10 each.

The 1975 season was no better for Chuck Tanner and the White Sox than the preceding one. Pitching was still strong with Kaat winning 20 and losing 14 while Wood won 16 and lost 20. Goose Gossage was the league's premier reliever with 26 saves. Bucky Dent, in his third year in the majors, proved to be one of the best shortstops in the league. Jorge Orta was the only .300 hitter (.306). With the departure of Allen and the slumping of Melton, May and Henderson, the slugging end of the Sox offense disappeared. Again it was a fifth-place finish, with an uninspiring record of 75-86.

Above: Bucky Dent broke into the majors with the White Sox in 1973. He became a starter the following year and held the job without challenge until he was traded to the Yankees in 1977. His best year at bat for the Sox was 1974 when he hit .274.

Rich "Goose" Gossage began his major league career in Chicago in 1972 and worked in the Sox bullpen through 1976, but his best years would be with the Yankees. As a member of the Sox, Gossage did have one excellent year, however, in 1975, when he led both leagues with 26 saves, and produced a 9-8 record and an ERA of 1.84.

Before the 1976 season began, a number of major White Sox figures would depart – Bill Melton to the California Angels, Jim Kaat to the Philadelphia Phillies, and Ken Henderson to the Atlanta Braves (but

for him they would get outfielder Ralph Garr). And shortly after the season began, Carlos May departed for the Yankees in exchange for pitcher Ken Brett.

Throughout the 1975 season there had been rumors that it might be the last one for the White Sox in Chicago. The team was up for sale and word was that the buyer might very well whisk it out of Chicago. At least the part about the club being for sale was true, John Allyn admitted. And who was there to buy it? None other than Bill Veeck, bidding to regain ownership of the organization he had given up in 1961. By December 1975 he accomplished it by organizing a syndicate of investors. The selling price was a reported $9.75 million.

Among the first and foremost things Veeck said while the deal was being put together was that he had no intention whatsoever of moving the Sox out of Chicago or Comiskey Park. That relieved the minds of most Sox fans. Now what they wanted was a repeat performance of Veeck's freshman year when he took over as owner back in 1959 – a pennant.

Above: Jim Kaat had 14 years experience when he came to the Sox in 1973, including a season when he was the league's ace hurler (1966: 25-13). In 1974, his first full year with the Sox, he topped 20 games for the second time (21-13), and followed the next year with a 20-14 season. As a Sox pitcher, Kaat won 45 games and lost 28 (.616).

Right: Terry Forster, a top reliever for the Sox in the early and mid-1970s, is mobbed after one of his 75 saves for the Sox. His two best years in Chicago were 1972, when he pulled out 29 games, and 1974, when his 24 saves were the most in the majors.

Left: Sox rightfielder Pat Kelly dives back to first and both he and the Minnesota Twins' Harmon Killebrew look expectantly for the umpire's call. Kelly was safe on this pickoff attempt by pitcher Bert Blyleven. Kelly played for the Sox from 1971 through 1976; his best year was 1974 when he batted .281 and stole 18 bases.

Below: Brian Downing was back-up catcher to Ed Herrmann in 1973 and 1974, took over the job full time for the next two years, then ceded it to Jim Essian before being traded to the California Angels. There, he would have his best year in 1979, batting .326.

Along with the return of the Veeck management came the return of manager Paul Richards for the 1976 season. Chuck Tanner had moved out west to lead the rival Oakland A's. Veeck and Richards could not, however, put anything together that year. Instead of a pennant, as Veeck had produced in his maiden year the first time around, the Sox staggered into the cellar of the AL West. They even lost 15 of the last 16 games of the season.

Even though the Sox were losing most of that year, the inveterate impresario Veeck turned Comiskey Park into an ongoing fiesta. To celebrate the American bicentennial, the theme of opening day at Comiskey Park was the "Spirit of '76." Veeck dressed in a tattered uniform, wore an antique wooden leg for the occasion, and marched with other would-be patriots in appropriate costumes. There was also Mexican night, Greek night, Family night, Teen night, Music night, even a German Oktoberfest. And during the season, he had Minnie Minoso put back on the roster as a player. The 53-year-old Minoso batted eight times and got one hit.

After that disappointing season, however, Veeck got down to the serious business of playing baseball. He hired Bob Lemon to manage the team. The Hall of Fame pitcher who had starred so long for the Cleveland Indians was given the directive to reverse the flow of the White Sox fortunes.

To help in that pursuit, the front office reached out for some power. With the absence of Allen, Melton and May, the Sox were virtually powerless. Richie Zisk, the slugging outfielder of the Pirates, was the first to be brought aboard. But it cost the Sox two of their ace relief pitchers, Goose Gossage and Terry Forster. To make up for that loss,

Left: Sox shortstop Bucky Dent is in the process of completing a double play against the Yankees in 1974. Looking on is former Cub Ron Santo who played the last year of his major league career across town with the Sox. The Yankee base runner is Graig Nettles.

Below: Paul Richards returned to manage the Sox in 1976 at the behest of new owner Bill Veeck. But it was hardly like old times. The Sox had a dismal season, 64-97 (.398), landing in the cellar of the American League West.

Above: Harry Caray was the voice of the White Sox from 1970 through 1981, when he moved across town to broadcast for the Cubs. The "Mayor of Rush Street," as he is also known, had a long career broadcasting with the St. Louis Cardinals before coming to the Sox.

Right: Jimmy Piersall, color commentator for White Sox broadcasts since 1977, became a key part of the new Sportsvision team instituted in 1981. Always outspoken, often controversial and most of the time walking a tightrope between the team management and his loyal listening audience, Piersall filled a variety of roles in telling the Sox story and in commenting on it.

the Sox obtained Lerrin LaGrow from the St. Louis Cardinals. From the re-entry draft that year the Sox picked up infielder Eric Soderholm and pitcher Steve Stone. Then, just before the regular season was to get underway, Veeck dealt shortstop Bucky Dent to the Yankees for another power hitter, outfielder Oscar Gamble. Alan Bannister would take over at short for the departed Dent and Jim Essian beat out Brian Downing for the job of catcher. Into the regular rotation would move two young right-handers, Francisco Barrios and Chris Knapp, as would southpaw Ken Kravec. It was a considerably different team from the one fielded by the Sox the previous year.

In 1977, the White Sox drew the largest single season attendance in their history, up to that time, a total of 1,657,135.

Above: Ralph Garr batted over .300 in three of his five years as a starter for the Atlanta Braves including a league-leading .353 in 1974, before coming to the Sox in 1976. Garr hit exactly .300 in each of his two years with the Sox, then dropped into the high .200s before being traded in 1979.

Right: The Sox first baseman for 1976 and 1977 was Jim Spencer who came from the Texas Rangers and then departed the Sox for the Yankees. Spencer tied Jorge Orta with 14 homers in '76 to lead the team, and hit another 18 the following year.

THE WHITE SOX
1977

Jim Spencer	1b
Jorge Orta	2b
Eric Soderholm	3b
Alan Bannister	ss
Richie Zisk	lf
Chet Lemon	cf
Ralph Garr	rf
Jim Essian	c
Oscar Gamble	dh
Steve Stone	p
Francisco Barrios	p
Chris Knapp	p
Ken Kravec	p
Lerrin LaGrow	p
Mgr. Bob Lemon	

Top right: Jim Essian was the Sox front-line catcher in 1976 and 1977, then, after a three-year interlude in Oakland, returned to serve as back-up for Carlton Fisk in 1981. Essian's best year was '77 when he hit .273, including 10 home runs.

Right: Lamar Johnson slides to break up a double play in this spring training game against the Pittsburgh Pirates. Leaping over him is second baseman Phil Garner. Johnson joined the Sox in 1974 and batted over .300 three times. His top average was .320 in 1976, and the following year he clouted a career-high 18 home runs.

Left: Bill Veeck holds court from a corner of the Bard's Room at Comiskey Park. Veeck's second session as Sox owner lasted from the 1976 season through 1980.

Below: When the Sox needed some power in 1977 they went to the National League for Richie Zisk. It cost them relief pitchers Terry Forster and Goose Gossage, but Zisk whacked 30 home runs and drove in 101 runs that year. They were unable to keep him the following year, however, and Zisk went to the Texas Rangers.

The trade for Zisk, questioned by many when it was perpetrated, lost much of its controversy on Opening Day 1977 when he slammed a home run on his first trip to the plate and then followed it with three more hits. By May 1st, Zisk had eight home runs. In fact, the entire White Sox offense gave evidence that it was definitely a revitalized entity. By June 19th, the Sox had moved into first place in the AL West, and even though it was by a minuscule two percentage points, it was a vast improvement over the last place performance the year before.

Veeck continued to entice people to the ballpark with a variety of gimmicks and give-aways, but it was basically the team's performance, especially the explosive attack from home plate, that was bringing the fans out with increasing regularity.

The competition for the Sox was coming principally from Whitey Herzog's Kansas City Royals. With hitters like George Brett, John Mayberry, Freddie Patek, Al Cowens, Amos Otis, Darrell Porter, and Hal McRae, they were a formidable opponent.

Still, the Sox hung in. By mid-July they were two-and-a-half games in front, and late in the month their lead had grown to five games. On July 30th, the White Sox topped the one million mark in home attendance, the first time in their 77-year history they had counted that many customers in Comiskey Park before August 1st. The entire season before, the club had only drawn 914,945.

In 1977, utility infielder Jack Brohamer hit for the cycle – single, double, triple, home run – in a game at Seattle. He was only the second Sox batter to accomplish that, the other being catcher Ray Schalk, who did it against the Tigers back in 1922.

Left: Oscar Gamble played one year in Chicago, 1977, and, when he wasn't tending to his hair, managed to lead the team in home runs with a total of 31. He also batted .297 and drove in 83 runs while serving much of the time as the club's designated hitter.

Below: Eric Soderholm played the keystone corner for the Sox from 1977 until he was traded in 1979. In his first season he cracked 25 home runs and batted .280; the following year he led the team with 20 fourbaggers.

Left: Bob Lemon managed the Sox to a third-place finish in 1977, but his team had slumped to fifth the following year when he left for the New York Yankees to replace Billy Martin. For his superb pitching career with the Cleveland Indians (1946-58, 207 wins and 128 losses, .618), Lemon was inducted into the Hall of Fame in 1976.

Above: Chet Lemon slides for the plate under a high-jumping catcher from the Toronto Blue Jays in this 1978 game. He was safe.

Right: After a long career with the Cubs, Don Kessinger eventually came to the South Side to play in the Sox infield. He played from 1977 into 1979. That last year he took over as player-manager but was replaced after 106 games, of which his team had won only 46. As a player, Kessinger, in his 16 years in the majors, appeared in 2,078 games and had a lifetime batting average of .252.

The lead began to pass back and forth in August between the Sox and the Royals, and at month's end the Sox were trailing by two games. September was a bad month for the Sox, but not for the Royals who steadily pulled away from the foundering Sox. When the season ended, the Sox had dropped to third place, 12 games behind the Royals.

The Sox set a new attendance record for Comiskey Park in 1977, 1,657,135. Those fans, if they lacked a pennant winner, had at least been entertained with the most home runs the Sox had hit in their history (192), a record that would stand until the Sox of 1996 clouted 195. Gamble led the team with 31, Zisk was a close second with 30. Eric Soderholm contributed 25; Chet Lemon, 19; Lamar Johnson and Jim Spencer, 18 each; Jorge Orta, 11; and Ralph Garr and Jim Essian, 10 apiece. Steve Stone had turned in the best Sox pitching performance with a 15-12 record. Francisco Barrios posted a record of 14-7. And Lerrin LaGrow proved to be a master fireman with 25 saves.

The Sox, however, could not keep that impressive ensemble together. At the start of the 1978 season, Zisk was in a Texas uniform. Gamble went over to the National League to join San Diego. The Sox traded for slugger Bobby Bonds, then traded him off to Texas, after a month, for Claudell Washington. The Sox picked up shortstop Don Kessinger, the long-time Cub star, but he was 35. The Sox also signed some promising young pitchers in Steve Trout (20), Ross Baumgarten (23), Rich Wortham (24), and Britt Burns (19).

Britt Burns was a product of the free agent draft of 1978. The 6'5" hurler was 19 years old when he made his Sox debut. By 1980 he was a key starter and turned in a fine rookie record of 15-13, with an ERA of 2.84. In '81 he again turned in the best mound performance for the Sox, winning 10 and losing six while maintaining a 2.64 ERA. Burns spent eight years with the Sox, and his finest was his last, 1985, 18-11 with a 3.96 ERA.

Wayne Nordhagen did just about everything for the White Sox in 1979. Here, putting the squash and a tag on a runner, he is a catcher, but he also played in the outfield, pitched two games and served as designated hitter that year. Nordhagen came up with the Sox in 1976 and hit .315 the next year and .301 the year after, playing in about a third of the games each year. In 1981, he was the Sox's leading hitter, with an average of .308.

The team was just not the same, however. The Sox were never a contender in the AL West in 1978. Midway through the season they lost manager Bob Lemon, who was wooed to New York to take over the Yankees after George Steinbrenner fired Billy Martin. Sox Coach Larry Doby moved up to lead the team for the rest of the year, but he could only win 37 of their remaining 87 games. The Sox ended up in fifth place, 20 1/2 games off pace. The team that had slammed 192 home runs the year before could only tally 106 in 1978. Their 634 runs that year were 210 less that what was produced in 1977.

Chet Lemon batted .300 and was the team leader. Eric Soderholm hit 20 home runs, and Jorge Orta and Chet Lemon had 13 apiece. Steve Stone was the premier pitcher, but his record was only 12-12.

In spite of the dismal season, the fans still came out to the ballpark. Opening Day set a record for that date at Comiskey Park when 50,754 showed up to cheer the Sox on. And after the last game of 1978 was played, the Sox could count 1,491,100 bodies who had passed through the turnstiles, the third highest then in club history.

For 1979, Don Kessinger was signed on as manager, becoming one of the few player-managers in modern baseball history. Soderholm, the team's mainstay at third, departed after two months for Texas, and the infield of the White Sox became a game of musical chairs as Alan Bannister, Greg Pryor, Kevin Bell, Jim Morrison, and Kessinger moved freely between second, shortsop, and third.

The Sox finished in fifth place that year, their record, (73-87 – .456), a slight improvement over the year before. But they had never threatened the California Angels who won the division crown that year.

There had been some credible performances. Chet Lemon batted .318, and his 44 doubles were most in the American League and the second highest then in Sox history (Floyd Robinson hit 45 in 1962). He also led the Sox in homers with 17. Lamar Johnson batted .309. And there seemed to be justifiable hope with the young pitching staff who had taken over the regular rotation – Ken Kravec (15-13), Rich Wortham (14-14), Ross Baumgarten (13-8), and Steve Trout (11-8). Ed Farmer was the bullpen ace; he had been obtained during the season from Texas and racked up 14 saves for the Sox.

Don Kessinger did not last the season, however. With a record of 46-60 he was replaced on an interim basis by Tony LaRussa who had been managing the Sox farm club, the Iowa Oaks. Under LaRussa, the Sox split the remainder of the season, winning 27 and losing 27.

Tony LaRussa had the distinction of being the youngest manager in the major leagues when he signed a contract with Bill Veeck to formally lead the team, but he was ancient compared to the ballplayers he was to manage. The White Sox were an especially young team. Wayne Nordhagen was the only starter over 29, and the pitching regulars were all veritable youngsters: Britt Burns, 21; Rich Dotson, 21; Steve Trout, 22; and LaMarr Hoyt, 25.

Mike Squires served as the Sox first baseman for most of the time from 1979 through 1984. His best year was 1980 when he hit .283. Squires spent his entire major league stint with the Sox and has a career batting average of .260.

Left: Tony LaRussa, arguing here, was managing the Iowa Oaks, a Sox farm club, in 1979 when he got the call to come to Chicago and lead the Sox through the remainder of that season. At 34, he was the youngest manager in the major leagues. Under LaRussa the Sox won 27 and lost 27 in '79, but the following year they could only win 70 for him while losing 90 to end up in fifth place in the American League West. LaRussa managed the Sox until he was fired during the 1986 season. He is the third winningest manager in Sox history, 522-510 (.504), including a division title in 1983.

Above: Utility infielder Greg Pryor came to the White Sox in 1978. His most fruitful year was 1979 when he batted .275.

Left: Rich Dotson donned a Sox uniform in late 1979 and produced a record of 2-0. The following year he moved into the rotation and won 12 and lost 10. Dotson came up with nine wins against eight losses in 1981. Dotson would prove to be one of the ace hurlers of the Sox through the 1980s.

Under LaRussa, the White Sox started strong and on May 1st, led the AL West with a record of 12-7. They dropped to second, then third later in the month, then regained the lead – for four days anyway. It was not until mid-June that the Sox began to have problems. Still they hung onto second place most of the time, although they were dropping farther and farther behind. By the All-Star break they were eight-and-a-half games out, with a record that had dissipated to 38-41.

The Kansas City Royals were the team to beat in the AL West, but nobody was doing it in 1980. The White Sox would lose eight of their 13 encounters with the Kansas City club that year. And the Royals glided easily into the division championship by totally dominating the second half of the season. The Sox, who battled respectably in the first half, sank to fifth place, a full 26 games behind the Royals.

Above: The Sox traded for infielder Jim Morrison in 1979, and he secured a full-time job at second base in 1980, when this photo was taken. Morrison batted a respectable .283 that year, including 15 home runs. In '81 he moved to third base and batted .235. Morrison left for the Pittsburgh Pirates in 1982.

Left: Rick Wortham had the best of his three years with the Sox in 1979 when he won 14 and lost 14. He left after the 1980 season for Oakland.

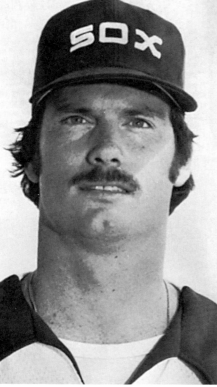

A typical Veeck-ism was wrought in October. Minnie Minoso, now 57, was activated and made two appearances at bat to ovations from nostalgic fans, but he went hitless in his two trips to the plate.

The Sox record for 1980, 70-90 (.438), was a large disappointment after the way they began the season. On the brighter side, however, Britt Burns showed definite potential as he led the Sox pitching staff with a record of 15-13 and an ERA of 2.84. Ed Farmer, who came out of the bullpen in 64 different games, was credited with 30 saves, a White Sox record at the time.

There was little hitting, however. Chet Lemon led the team with a .292 average, and first baseman Mike Squires and secondbagger Jim Morrison each hit .283. Outfielder Harold Baines had the longest hitting streak of the season, 11 consecutive games. In the area of slugging, Morrison and Wayne Nordhagen knocked 15 homers each, and Morrison hit 40 doubles, far and away the most for the Sox that year.

The White Sox's new owners of 1981, Eddie Einhorn (left) and Jerry Reinsdorf, flanked Chicago's Mayor Jane Byrne, whom they hoped to convert into a loyal baseball fan. (Photo courtesy of the *City of Chicago.*)

Bill Veeck would not be with the White Sox in 1981. The team was up for sale, and there was interest from a variety of concerns. The haggling and the wheeling and dealing had been going on throughout the 1980 season. The Sox Board of Directors had approved the sale of the club to self-made multi-millionaire Edward DeBartolo of Cincinnati who promised to keep the franchise in Chicago. But among other American League owners, baseball commissioner Bowie Kuhn, and American League president Lee MacPhail, approval of the sale was denied. The grounds cited were that DeBartolo owned interests in other professional sports organizations, which was against major league rules.

So the White Sox were put on the bargaining block again, and this time there was a partnership that the American League would approve. The Sox were sold to Jerry Reinsdorf and Eddie Einhorn for a reported $20 million. The team would stay in Chicago, and they would be improved as a team, the new owners promised. Reasonably, they said, it would take a little time, but they were committed to building a winner. The 1981 season, with its two-month players strike and split season would, however, prove counterproductive to their efforts.

Still, the 1981 season got off to a very exciting start for the Sox and their new owners, who had illustrated they were as intent as they had said about improving the team. Offense was the obvious place to begin. So, to beef up the anemic hitting of the Sox, they went to Boston and acquired longtime star catcher Carlton Fisk. He had played with the Red Sox since he came up from the minors in 1971. A Rookie of the Year in 1972, Fisk was a designated starter in five All-Star games and played in two others as well. He had a lifetime batting average of .281 when he joined the White Sox and was an acknowledged clutch slugger.

For additional power they signed gargantuan first baseman Greg "Bull" Luzinski, who had played with the Phillies the year before. A two-time runner-up for the American League MVP award, Luzinski had hit more than 30 home runs three times and drove in more than 100 runs three times. The Sox also traded Ken Kravec to the crosstown Cubs for right-hander Dennis Lamp.

On opening day, the Reinsdorf/Einhorn Sox trotted out onto the field at Fenway Park in

The 5,000th White Sox home run was hit September 2, 1981, at Comiskey Park by Chet Lemon.

Above: Chet Lemon was one of the best hitters for the White Sox from 1978 through 1981. He joined the Sox in 1975 and became a regular in center field the following year. He hit .300 or better three times in his last four years, his best effort being in 1979 when he hit .318, including 44 doubles, the league high and only one short of the then Sox record. Lemon hit .302 in 1981, and was traded after the season to Detroit for slugging outfielder, Steve Kemp.

Left: LaMarr Hoyt commuted between the White Sox and their farm clubs in 1979 and 1980 before arriving for a full, if abbreviated, season in 1981. That year he won nine and lost only three, with an ERA of 3.22. But his best years in a Sox uniform were yet to come.

Above: A rookie in 1980, Harold Baines found full-time work in right field. He batted .255 that year, and followed in '81 with an average of .286. He was destined to become the Sox's most stellar hitter of the 1980s.

Above: Steve "Rainbow" Trout moved from the minors to the Sox in 1979 and promptly won 11 big-league games while losing only eight. He turned around a poor 1980 season (9-16) in 1981 by winning eight and losing seven. He left the Sox for the Chicago Cubs after the 1982 season.

Left: Shortstop Bill Almon was not even a roster player going into the 1981 season but managed to win a starting job and then turned out a performance as the best - hitting shortstop in baseball that year, with an average of .301. Almon hit .256 for the Sox in 1982 and then departed for Oakland.

Boston under the field generalship of Tony LaRussa. It was Carlton Fisk's first major league appearance in a uniform that did not bear the emblem of the Red Sox. Against his former teammates, he demonstrated the extent of their loss by blasting a three-run homer to give the White Sox a 5-3 win.

Back in Chicago to open the home season, there was expansive excitement. A record crowd for opening day in Comiskey Park turned out, 51,560. And if it was Carlton Fisk they came to see, he rewarded them with a grand slam home run in the fourth inning to spur the Sox to a 9-3 win over the Milwaukee Brewers.

In April, the Sox put together a six-game winning streak and were off to an exciting start. By the end of the month they boasted a record of 11-6. The pace in the American League West was being set by the Sox, the Oakland A's, and the Texas Rangers.

Below: Greg Luzinski, 6'1", 225 pounds, twice a runner-up for the MVP award when he was with the Phillies in the National League, was one of the game's premier power hitters in the 1970s. During his first year with the Sox, 1981, he became the team's focal point, hitting 21 home runs in 106 games and driving in 62 runs, far and away the best slugging effort on the club that year. He hit 32 home runs for the Sox in 1983, and retired after the 1984 season with a career total of 307 home runs and a batting average of .276.

Above: Acquiring Carlton Fisk, the longtime star catcher for the Red Sox, in 1981, was the first step in upgrading the Sox line-up by new owners Eddie Einhorn and Jerry Reinsdorf. A Rookie of the Year (1972) and a regular in many All-Star games, Fisk held numerous Red Sox records for batting and fielding. Coming to the Sox, Fisk carried a career average of .284 and a total of 162 homers. His 1981 production for the Sox was below that average output – .263 and seven home runs. He would become a Sox legend over the ensuing 12 seasons in Chicago.

When the month of May ended, the Sox were 26-18 and a very definite division contender. Rich Dotson was having a fine year and by the second week in June had posted four shutouts. But then came the players' strike and all ballparks in the major leagues were emptied. It lasted until early August, when the season resumed on a split schedule that would involve a unique set of playoffs at the end of the year. They would not affect the White Sox, however, because Part Two of the 1981 season was a dismal one. From a contender just two-and-a-half games out of first at the end of Part One of the season, the Sox plummeted to sixth place in the second half, winning only 23 games while losing 30 (.434).

Before the second half of the season got underway, the Sox played a city series of two games with the Cubs for charity, reviving memories of the long tradition of intra-city exhibition games that expired in World War II. The first game ended in a 0-0 tie at Comiskey Park and the second game was won by the Cubs, 4-3, at Wrigley Field.

The Sox picked up lefthanded pitcher Jerry Koosman from the Minnesota Twins during the season's second half. The staff he would join was led again by Britt Burns who won 10 and lost six, although

Dennis Lamp came up with the best ERA, 2.41. But the most fireworks of the strange 1981 season came from the bat of Greg Luzinski who powered 21 homers in the shortened season and drove in 62 runs. The Sox also had three .300 hitters – Wayne Nordhagen (.308), Chet Lemon (.302), and Bill Almon (.301).

When the season ended, owners Eddie Einhorn and Jerry Reinsdorf promised that there were new things to come, for the team and for the fans. Their administration was going to be an active one, an aggressive one, they said. The White Sox of the '80s were going to be a team to watch.

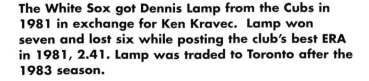

The White Sox got Dennis Lamp from the Cubs in 1981 in exchange for Ken Kravec. Lamp won seven and lost six while posting the club's best ERA in 1981, 2.41. Lamp was traded to Toronto after the 1983 season.

Left: Deft base thief Ron LeFlore came to the Sox from the Montreal Expos in 1981 where he had led the National League in stolen bases with 97 the year before. During the five years before that, he starred for the Detroit Tigers, his best year being 1976 when he batted .316 and led the American League in base thefts with 58. In a Sox uniform in '81, he increased his career total of stolen bases above the 400 mark. He batted .287 for the Sox in 1982, and retired after the season.

Below: The White Sox of 1981. Left to right: Back row – LaMarr Hoyt, Francisco Barrios, Steve Trout, Greg Luzinski, Carlton Fisk, Wayne Nordhagen, Lamar Johnson, Rusty Kuntz, Ed Farmer; Third row – Dewey Robinson, Rich Dotson, Greg Pryor, Harold Baines, Chet Lemon, Bob Molinaro, Ross Baumgarten, Jim Morrison, Todd Cruz; Second row – Herman Schneider (trainer), Mike Squires, Bill Almon, Glen Rosenbaum (traveling secretary), Ron LeFlore, Jim Essian, Marc Hill, Willie Thompson (equipment manager), Carl Homes (bat boy); Front row – Dennis Lamp, Art Kusnyer (coach), Dave Nelson (coach), Ron Schueler (coach), Vada Pinson (coach), Tony LaRussa (manager), Bobby Winkles (coach), Kevin Hickey, Tony Bernazard, Tony McQuery (bat boy), John McNamara (equipment manager).

5
The
Modern Era

The year 1983 was an auspicious one in Chicago White Sox lore because a new age began to take shape at Comiskey Park. It marked the beginning of an exciting roller coaster ride that would carry on into the 1990s. The era would bring into focus some of the finest and most productive ballplayers in White Sox history, and a modern new ballpark would be built to showcase them.

Coming off a third-place finish in 1982, the White Sox surged through the American League West, winning 99 games against only 63 losses, the second most victories in club history, eclipsed only by the 100 wins posted by the 1917 World Series champion Sox. At season's end Chicago stood 20 games ahead of second-place Kansas City in the American League West, a record margin in major league history. The team's 800 runs scored was a league high.

Tom Paciorek turned in the best batting average with a .307 and Ron Kittle provided the most power leading the club with 35 home runs and 100 RBIs. Rudy Law set a team record by stealing 77 bases, still the most thefts ever in Sox history. LaMarr Hoyt led all American League pitchers with a record of 24-10, and Rich Dotson turned in a 22-7 season (.857, the fifth highest win percentage in Sox history) and logged the team's best ERA at 3.23.

The Sox met the Baltimore Orioles to determine the 1983 AL

pennant and jumped in front at Baltimore in Game One with a 2-1 triumph on the arm of LaMarr Hoyt. Then a collapse as surprising as it was awful: the Sox scored only one run in the next three games, falling to the Orioles 4-0 in Baltimore and 11-1 and 3-0 back home at Comiskey Park.

In that otherwise memorable year, the White Sox also played host to the golden anniversary of the major league All-Star Game. The very first All-Star classic had been played in Comiskey Park 50 years earlier to the day (July 6). In that premier All-Star Game outfielder Al Simmons and third baseman Jimmy Dykes represented the White Sox; in 1983 left fielder Ron Kittle was the lone selectee. And it was the first time in club history that attendance at Comiskey Park topped the two million mark (2,132,821 – for trivia buffs, the White Sox first exceeded one million in 1951 [1,328,234]).

Catcher Carlton Fisk was truly the White Sox man of the '80s, starring from 1981 on into the '90s. When he ended his baseball career after 1,421 games in a White Sox uniform (only six Sox have played in more), he held the Sox career home run record with 214 (since surpassed by Frank Thomas). His other career rankings of note in Sox annals are: Extra Base Hits, 442; 20 plus Home Run Seasons, 4, (fourth best); RBIs 762 (fifth); Total Bases, 2,143 (sixth); Hits, 1,259 and Doubles, 214, (10th). (Photo courtesy of *Photography By Schuth.*)

AMERICAN LEAGUE WEST CHAMPIONSHIP
1983

Game	R	H	E	Pitchers
Game 1 (10/5/83 at Baltimore)				
White Sox	2	7	0	Hoyt
Orioles	1	5	1	McGregor, Stewart, T. Martinez
Game 2 (10/6/83 at Baltimore)				
White Sox	0	5	2	Bannister, Barojas, Lamp
Orioles	4	6	0	Boddiker
Game 3 (10/7/83 at Comiskey Park)				
Orioles	11	8	1	Flanagan, Stewart
White Sox	1	6	1	Dotson, Tidrow, Koosman, Lamp
Game 4 (10/8/83 at Comiskey Park)				
Orioles	3	9	0	Davis, T. Martinez
White Sox	0	10	0	Burns, Barojas, Agosto, Lamp

LaMarr Hoyt hurled for the Sox from 1979 through 1984. He had two league-leading seasons, 1983 (24-10) and 1982 (19-15), and was honored with the Cy Young Award in '83. His winning percentage of .602 is fifth best in Sox history. Hoyt won a total of 74 games for the Sox while losing 49 and had a Sox career ERA of 3.96.

On May 16, 1984, in a game with the Kansas City Royals, Carlton Fisk became the third player in team history to hit for the cycle. The others were Ray Schalk on June 22, 1922, against the Detroit Tigers, and Jack Brohamer on September 24, 1977, against the Seattle Mariners.

Slugger Ron Kittle added power to the Sox lineup in two segments, 1982-86 and 1989-91. Kittle is fifth on the ballclub's all-time home run list with 140; the 35 he hit in 1983 stood as the second most in club history until the Frank Thomas era. Kittle hit another 32 homers in 1984 and 26 in 1985.

As quickly as the White Sox rose to pennant contention, they also fell. Despite fielding much the same team, the 1984 Sox skidded to a fifth-place tie with Seattle in the AL West, their 74-88 record leaving them 10 games behind the Kansas City Royals. LaMarr Hoyt slumped to a 13-18 record, while Tom Seaver, acquired from the Cincinnati Reds before the season, turned in a stellar 15-11, and Floyd Bannister won 14 while losing only 11. Rich Dotson repeated with the best ERA, 3.59. Harold Baines was the only hitter above .300 (.304) and led the team with 94 RBIs. Ron Kittle again banged the most home runs, 32, and Baines added another 29. Still it was a major disappointment after the hope engendered by the '83 Sox.

There was, however, one truly unforgettable game; it lasted two days, in fact. On May 8, the Sox took on the Milwaukee Brewers at Comiskey Park in a contest which was not decided until May 9 when Harold Baines finally homered in the bottom of the 25th inning to give the Sox a 7-6 victory. It stands as the longest game in major league history, 8 hours and 6 minutes, and the most number of innings ever in an American League game.

The roller coaster headed back up track in 1985. Manager Tony LaRussa began his seventh season at the helm (only Jimmy Dykes and Al Lopez can claim longer managerial tenures with the Sox). It was also the 75th anniversary of the venerable Comiskey Park, the oldest in the major leagues, which had been formally opened as White Sox Park on July 1, 1910.

Kansas City was still the team to beat in the American League West and the California Angels were also considered a legitimate contender for the division title. Hoyt and Dotson were absent from the pitching rotation in 1985. Britt Burns turned in the best record of the season, 18-11, and newcomer Gene Nelson was 10-10. Seaver, who was credited with his 300th win on August 4 against the Yankees (only 20 pitchers in major league history have won that many games), was 16-11 for the year and posted the best ERA, 3.17.

Once again Baines was the only .300 hitter (.309), including 22 home runs and a team-high 113 RBIs. Carlton Fisk tied the club record with 37 home runs set by Dick Allen in 1972, and added another 107 RBIs. And Ozzie Guillen had the distinction of being the American League's top fielding shortstop with an average of .980. However, despite their 85 wins against 77 losses, the White Sox could climb no higher than third place in 1985, six games behind Kansas City and five below California.

After that brief rise, the White Sox were destined to plunge again, this time following a sub-.500 track that would last for the remainder of the decade. In 1986 LaRussa made it only 20 days into June before he was fired and replaced by Doug Rader for two games and then Jim Fregosi for the remainder of the season. The Sox ended up 72-90 and in fifth place that year.

No one on the Sox batted .300 in 1986. Baines' .296 marked the top, as did his 21 homers and 88 RBIs. Rich Dotson was back but he had the ignominious distinction of tying for the most losses in the American League that year, 17 against only 10 wins. The best pitching record was logged by Joe Cowley, 11-11, in his only year in a White Sox uniform.

After the season ended Ken Harrelson was replaced as general manager by Larry Himes. Five weeks later, the only true highlight of the year came not from the ballclub but from the State of Illinois General Assembly which passed funding legislation to build a new ballpark for the White Sox.

1987 was much the same. The Sox landed in fifth place again, this time with a record of 77-85. Baines gave up his right field position to Ivan Calderon but as the Sox designated hitter he shared the team batting title with Calderon, both posting averages of .293. Calderon hit the most home runs, 28, while Gene Walker drove in the most runs, 94. Floyd Bannister won 16 games while losing 11 and had the leading

Ivan Calderon roamed the outfield for the White Sox from 1986 to 1990 and then again in 1993. His best season was 1987 when he shared the batting title with Harold Baines (both hit .293) and led the club with 28 home runs. During his career with the White Sox, Calderon hit 70 home runs and drove in 279 runs.

ERA at 3.58, but Dotson and Jose DeLeon each posted disappointing records of 11-12.

With Fregosi working his second full (and last) season as pilot, the Sox in 1988 stumbled through their third consecutive fifth-place season, winning only 71 games while losing 90, a dismal and distant 32 1/2 games out of first, the farthest back since 1948 when the club's 51-101 season left them 44 1/2 games behind. The only real highlight of the year came on July 22 when Baines whacked his 154th home run as a White Sox player to break the career record held by Bill Melton since 1975. Newcomer Dave Gallagher became the first player to hit above .300 for the Sox in several years (.303). Only one player, Dan Pasqua, hit 20 home runs, and just one drove in more than 50 runs, designated hitter Harold Baines (81). Jerry Reuss, acquired from the Los Angeles Dodgers, led all pitchers with a 13-9 record and a 3.44 ERA; Melido Perez was 12-10. After the season Fregosi was dismissed and the managerial job was bestowed on Jeff Torborg.

On May 7, 1989, Sox owners and a coterie of celebrities, headed by Illinois Governor Jim Thompson and Chicago Mayor Richard M. Daley, broke ground for the new Comiskey Park to be built just across 35th Street from the old one. The new home for the White Sox was scheduled to open for the 1991 season. But things only got worse in 1989 and the Sox ended up in the cellar of the American League West, their record of 69-92 the poorest since 1976 when they won only 64 games. The only pitcher to post a winning record was Reuss, 8-5. Reliever Bobby Thigpen, however, set a then-club record with 34 saves. Designated hitter Baines batted a career-high .321 with the Sox but was traded in August to the Texas Rangers, while Carlos Martinez hit .300 on the head.

With the turn of the decade, however, the White Sox roller coaster took a significant turn upwards. Over was the four-year slump of losing seasons. Not only was it over but the 1990 Sox chalked up their best record since winning the division back in 1983. With 94 wins against 64 losses, they moved up to second place in the AL West behind the Oakland A's who won 103 games (and would take their third consecutive American League pennant under former Sox manager Tony LaRussa).

In the lineup, two star-destined young men made their debuts in White Sox uniforms, pitcher Jack McDowell and first baseman Frank

Thomas. McDowell shared the team's best pitching record in 1990 with Greg Hibbard, 14-9, while Thomas hit .330 in 191 at-bats. The two were touted by the city's sportswriters as the linchpins to secure a divisional title . . . perhaps a pennant . . . maybe a world's championship.

Thigpen claimed a club record for saves in 1990 with 57, a new American League standard as well. And Carlton Fisk on August 17 in a game against the Texas Rangers, set an all-time major league record for home runs by a catcher, his 328th, surpassing the mark held by Hall of Famer Johnny Bench. It was also his 187th as a White Sox, which took the club record from Harold Baines. The previous year he had logged another major league milestone when he collected his 2,000th hit.

The White Sox played their last game at the old Comiskey Park on September 30, 1990. Appropriately enough, they won, defeating the Seattle Mariners 2-1, closing out a collective record of 3,024 wins against 2,926 losses (.508) in the grand old stadium.

Bobby Thigpen is credited with more saves than any Sox reliever in history, chalking up 201 during his eight-year career in Chicago (1986-93). The 57 he logged in 1990 is 19 more than second-ranked Roberto Hernandez who saved 38 in both 1993 and 1996. Thigpen also holds the club record for saves in a single month (13).

A day of historic significance to Sox fans of long-standing, September 30, 1990, the last game in the old Comiskey Park. The White Sox defeated Seattle 2-1, to bring their 80-year record in the venerable old stadium to 3,024 wins-2,926 losses (.508). (Photo courtesy of *Photography By Schuth.*)

Left: Jack McDowell throws the first pitch here in the new Comiskey Park, April 18, 1981, against the Tigers. The batter is Detroit's Tony Phillips, and the Sox catcher is Carlton Fisk. The pitch, a fastball, was called a ball. (Photo courtesy of *Photography By Schuth.*)

Below: The new Comiskey Park is officially opened April 18, 1991 with guests of honor Chicago Mayor Richard M. Daley and Illinois Governor James Thompson in attendance. The new stadium attracted a club-record 2,934,154 fans in its first year. (Photo courtesy of *Photography By Schuth.*)

The new Comiskey Park opened on April 18, 1991, with a crowd of 42,191 fans gathered to watch the less-than-auspicious christening of the new White Sox home. The Detroit Tigers drubbed the Sox that afternoon 16-0. Four days later, however, the White Sox fared better in the first night game played in the new ballpark, a game in which Frank Thomas hit the first home run there to help the Sox defeat the Baltimore Orioles. The most dramatic game of the season, however, occurred on August 11 when rookie hurler Wilson Alvarez, in his first appearance for the White Sox and only his second major league start, threw a no-hitter to defeat the Orioles 7-0 in Baltimore.

The 1991 White Sox, with a record of 87-75, could not get beyond second place again, finishing eight games behind Minnesota. Thomas, the designated hitter that year, led the team with a batting average of .318, 32 home runs and 109 RBIs. Robin Ventura also distinguished himself by hitting .284 with 23 homers and 100 RBIs. McDowell won 17 games and lost only 11 and he had the best ERA, 3.41; Greg Hibbard was 11-11. The organization had to find certain pleasure, however, in the fact that more fans turned out to watch the White Sox in 1991 than in any other year in history. A total of 2,934,154 filled the new Comiskey Park, almost 800,000 more than the previous record attendance for a single season. After back-to-back second-place seasons, however, Jeff Torborg resigned as manager, and the Sox front office chose Gene Lamont to replace him for the 1992 season.

Jack McDowell debuted with the White Sox in 1987 but inscribed his mark on team history from 1990 through 1993, leading the pitching staff in each of those four years and becoming the first Sox hurler to produce back-to-back 20-game winning seasons (20-10 in 1992 and 22-10 in 1993) since Jim Kaat in 1974-75. McDowell was also the first Sox pitcher to win the Cy Young Award (1993) since LaMarr Hoyt in 1983.

Below: Lance Johnson won the center field job with the Sox in 1990 and held it down through the 1995 season. His best year with the Sox was his last, when he hit .306 and led the American League with 186 hits. Also in 1995 Johnson tied a major league mark by collecting six hits in a nine-inning game (against the Twins at the Metrodome) and set another White Sox record with three triples in that game.

The Sox ride took a brief decline in Lamont's inaugural year at the helm, dropping to third place in the American League West. It was, however, a most impressive year for both Frank Thomas and Jack McDowell. Thomas batted .323, the highest average recorded by a White Sox hitter since Minnie Minoso's .324 in 1951, and drove in 115 runs, the most since Minoso logged 116 in 1954. Thomas' 24 home runs were second in 1992, however, to the 25 whacked by designated hitter George Bell. McDowell (20-10) became the team's first 20-game winner since LaMarr Hoyt and Rich Dotson won 24 and 22 respectively in 1983, and he led the club with an ERA of 3.18. Robin Ventura hit .282, including 16 homers, a career-high 38 doubles, and 93 RBIs.

Above: Gene Lamont piloted the Sox from 1992 until he was replaced by Terry Bevington in 1995. His 258 victories rank 10th in the Sox managerial record book, and his winning percentage of .551 is the sixth best. In the three years he was full-time manager, Lamont's teams won the division in 1993 and were leading it when the 1994 season was prematurely ended by a players' strike.

The 1993 season proved to be a much more memorable one. It was a year of a variety of notable events. Bo Jackson, becoming the first major-leaguer to play with an artificial hip, led it off with a home run on his first swing of the year. Tim Raines became only the second hitter in Sox history to homer from both sides of the plate in the same game, and became the fourth top base-stealer in major-league history. Thomas demolished the club home-run record held by Harold Baines and Carlton Fisk (37) by hitting 41. And the Sox took the division title, their first since 1983, by eight games with a record of 94-68.

Once again Thomas was the leading batter, .317, and the 128 runs he drove in stood second only in club annals to Zeke Bonura's 138 back in 1936. McDowell posted the best pitching record in the American League, 22-10, while Wilson Alvarez claimed the team's best ERA, 2.95, the first below 3.00 since Dennis Lamp in 1981.

In search of their first American League pennant since 1959, the Sox faced the Toronto Blue Jays, and in the first postseason game ever to be played in the new Comiskey Park, the Sox fell to Toronto 7-3. The following day they lost again 3-1. In Game Three in Toronto, however, behind the pitching of Wilson Alvarez, the Sox prevailed, 6-1. The next day they tied the series with a 7-4 victory, Tim Belcher getting the win. After that, however, the Sox still could not salvage a victory, losing the pennant with back-to-back losses of 5-3 in Toronto and 6-3 at Comiskey Park.

THE WHITE SOX
American League West Champions
1993

Frank Thomas	1b
Joey Cora	2b
Robin Ventura	3b
Ozzie Guillen	ss
Lance Johnson	cf
Tim Raines	lf
Ellis Burks	rf
Ron Karkovice	c
George Bell	dh
Wilson Alvarez	p
Jason Bere	p
Alex Fernandez	p
Jack McDowell	p
Roberto Hernandez	p
Mgr. Gene Lamont	

Alex Fernandez hurled for the White Sox from 1990 through 1996 before departing for the National League Florida Marlins. In 1996, Fernandez became only the fifth pitcher in Sox history to strike out 200 batters in a season, and he led the ballclub with a 16-10 record (fifth best in the American League), an ERA of 3.45 (fourth best) and in innings pitched, 258 (second most). In 1995 he also led the team with a record of 12-8 and an ERA of 3.80 as well as in innings pitched 203.2. His career stats with the Sox: 79-63, ERA of 3.78, 1,346.1 innings pitched and 951 strikeouts.

AMERICAN LEAGUE WEST CHAMPIONSHIP
1993

Game	R	H	E	Pitchers
Game 1 (10/5/96 at Comiskey Park)				
Blue Jays	7	17	1	Guzman, Cox, Ward
White Sox	3	6	1	McDowell, DeLeon, Radinsky, McCaskill
Game 2 (10/6/93 at Comiskey Park)				
Blue Jays	3	8	0	Stewart, Leiter, Ward
White Sox	1	7	2	Fernandez, Hernandez
Game 3 (10/8/93 at Toronto)				
White Sox	6	12	0	Alvarez
Blue Jays	1	7	1	Hentgen, Cox, Eichorn, Castillo
Game 4 (10/9/93 at Toronto)				
White Sox	7	11	0	Bere, Belcher, McCaskill, Radinsky Hernandez
Blue Jays	4	9	0	Stottlemyre, Leiter, Timlin
Game 5 (10/10/93 at Toronto)				
White Sox	3	5	1	McDowell, DeLeon, Radinsky, Hernandez
Blue Jays	5	14	0	Guzman, Castillo, Ward
Game 6 (10/12/93 at Comiskey Park)				
Blue Jays	6	10	0	Stewart, Ward
White Sox	3	5	3	Fernandez, McCaskill, Radinsky, Hernandez

Wilson Alvarez hurled a no-hitter in 1991 against the Baltimore Orioles in his first start for the White Sox and his second in the major leagues. He also shares with LaMarr Hoyt the Sox record for the longest winning streak for a pitcher (15 games, 1993-94). His best year so far with the Sox was 1993 when he posted a record of 15-8 and an ERA of 2.95.

The White Sox of 1993 celebrate their first division championship in a decade after defeating Seattle 4-2 on September 27, 1993. The decider was a three-run homer from the bat of Bo Jackson. (Photo courtesy of *Photography By Schuth.*)

The Big Hurt, Frank Thomas, has virtually rewritten the slugging section of the Sox record books since he joined the ballclub in 1990. He has the most career home runs (222) and the highest slugging average (.599) and his .327 batting average ranks third behind Shoeless Joe Jackson and Eddie Collins. Thomas is the only player in major league history to bat .300 or better with at least 20 home runs, 100 RBIs, 100 walks and 100 runs scored in six consecutive seasons, 1991-96, (closest to that achievement are Lou Gehrig and Ted Williams who each accomplished it, but only in four years). His batting average of .353 in 1994 and .349 in 1996 were the highest logged by any Sox batter since Luke Appling set the club record with .388 in 1936. He was the American League's MVP in 1993 and 1994, the first player in the American League to win that honor in consecutive years since Yankee Roger Maris did it back in 1961-62.

The year 1994 lives forever in baseball infamy, stopped two-thirds of the way through one of the most exciting seasons in ages by a players' strike and the first cancellation of a World Series since 1904. It was especially frustrating for White Sox fans. The team was in first place in the American League Central Division when play came to a halt after the August 11 games, and slugger Frank Thomas was in hot pursuit of the fabled triple crown, batting .353 with 38 home runs and 101 RBIs. Jason Bere was the top American League pitcher with a record of 12-2, and Lance Johnson led both leagues with 14 triples. The Sox also had two other .300 hitters, Julio Franco (.319) and Darrin Jackson (.312), and Franco also counted 20 home runs and drove in 98 runs while Robin Ventura contributed another 18 homers and 78 RBIs. Rounding out a winning pitching rotation, Wilson Alvarez was 12-8, Alex Fernandez 11-7, and McDowell 10-9. But the hopes for individual honors and perhaps a long-sought pennant and World Series appearance were doused with the early season closure.

Right: Shortstop Ozzie Guillen was a runaway for the American League Rookie of the Year honor when he joined the Sox in 1985. Since then his career stats with the team rank him fifth in games played (1,601), sixth in at-bats (5,577), seventh in hits (1,488), tenth in doubles (219), and his batting average going into the 1997 season stood at .267. Guillen's single-season fielding average for a White Sox shortstop of .981 in 1996 is second only to Ron Hansen's .983 in 1963.

Left: Reliever Roberto Hernandez has been the mainstay of the Sox bullpen of the 1990s. Joining the team in 1992, he has led the ballclub in saves every year since, recording career highs of 38 in both 1993 and 1996 (second only to Bobby Thigpen's Sox record of 57). His 1.91 ERA in 1996 was the league's best for a relief pitcher.

The top stolen base efficiency in White Sox history was registered in 1983 when Sox speedsters stole 165 bases on 215 attempts for a percentage of 76.7. Next best is the 1958 "Go-Go" Sox who stole 101 on 134 tries for 75.4 percent. And third is the 1995 Sox with 110 steals in 149 attempts for 73.8 percent.

Versatile third baseman Robin Ventura tied a major league record in 1995 when he became only the eighth player ever to hit two grand slam home runs in a game (against the Rangers at Texas). He ranks fifth in career homers for the Sox with 144, and the 34 he hit in 1996 were the most in a single season in team history by a left-handed batter. Ventura leads all major league third basemen of the 1990s in RBIs (563), runs scored (494), games played (842) and putouts (842); he ranks third in home runs (139) and batting average (.282). Ventura has also won four Golden Glove awards: 1991,1992,1993 & 1996.

On September 4, 1995, against the Texas Rangers, Robin Ventura tied a club record by driving in eight runs. Over the years only three others have also logged eight RBIs in one game: Carl Reynolds in 1930, Tommy McCraw in 1967 and Jim Spencer (twice) in 1977.

With good reason, the anticipation of White Sox fans was high when the players came back and the owners opened the stadiums for the 1995 season. But the Sox got off to a start as surprising as it was disappointing; by the end of May they were mired in fourth place in the five-team AL Central with an 11-19 record, 10 games out of first. On June 2, manager Gene Lamont was fired and replaced by Terry Bevington. The season, however, did not improve much for the Sox. It was not until September that the club was able to struggle up to third place in the division, and ended 32 games behind Cleveland and 30 back of Kansas City.

There were two games in 1995, however, that would go down in the Sox record book. On September 4 against the Rangers down in Texas, Robin Ventura tied a major league record when he became only the eighth player in history to hit two grand slam home runs in one game. His eight RBIs that day also tied the club record. Then, on September 23 in a game at Minnesota, Lance Johnson tied a major league record when he collected six hits in a nine-inning game. He also set a White Sox record with three triples in that game.

Thomas led the White Sox in hitting for the fifth consecutive year in 1995 with a batting average of .308. He also led the team in home runs (40), RBIs (111), runs scored (102), doubles (27, shared with Ray Durham), total bases (299), extra-base hits (67), walks (136), and slugging percentage (.606). Dave Martinez batted .307 while Lance Johnson hit .306, and Robin Ventura accounted for 26 home runs and 93 RBIs. Alex Fernandez was the only regular starter with a winning record for the Sox, 12-8, and he had the best ERA at 3.80, while reliever Roberto Hernandez accounted for 32 saves.

The roller coaster took a decided run toward the sky again in 1996, turning a losing 1995 season into a winning one, 85-77. Still, at season's end, the Sox trailed the Cleveland Indians, as they had all year, ending up in second place in the American League Central, 14 1/2 games behind.

Below: After 10 illustrious seasons as a member of the White Sox, Harold Baines' number 3 was honorarily retired by the organization in 1989, but it had to be brought out of retirement when he returned to the team as the designated hitter in 1996. Baines is the third most productive home run hitter in Sox history after Frank Thomas and Carlton Fisk, with a total of 208 through the 1996 season. His 296 doubles trail only Luke Appling (440) and Nellie Fox (335) in the club record book, and his 1,652 hits are the fourth best by a White Sox batter. In 1996, as designated hitter, he batted .311 with 22 homers, 95 RBIs and 80 runs scored.

Above: Tony Phillips joined the Sox outfield in 1996 after eight seasons with Oakland in the 1980s, then five with the Tigers and one with California in the '90s. One of the most feared leadoff hitters in the game, he was second in the American League in on-base percentage in his premier year with the Sox with a mark of .403, and led the league in walks with 125. Phillips batted .277 in 1996, ten percentage points above his career average, and scored 119 runs.

In 1996, Thomas batted .349, the highest in a full season (Thomas hit .353 in the strike-shortened 1994 season) since Luke Appling set the club all-time record of .388 in 1936. He also led in home runs with 40, one shy of the team record he set in 1993, and in RBIs, his 134 put him just four short of Zeke Bonura's club record also set in 1936. Thomas' .626 slugging average was bettered only once in Sox history when he slugged .729 in the strike-shortened 1994 season.

Dave Martinez was second in hitting with .318. Designated hitter Harold Baines batted .311 with 22 homers and 95 RBIs. Robin Ventura had 34 home runs and drove in 105 runs, Danny Tartabull had 27 fourbaggers and 101 RBIs. Tony Phillips led the team with 119 runs scored, and Ray Durham hit the most doubles, 33, while Ozzie Guillen and Martinez bagged the most triples, eight.

Above: Dave Martinez collected his 1,000th hit in August 1996 during a season which proved to be his finest at the plate in 10 years in the major leagues. He established career highs in '96 with a batting average of .318, 140 hits, 85 runs scored, 53 RBIs and 140 total bases. Martinez came to the White Sox in 1995 after stints in the National League with the Cubs, Montreal, Cincinnati and San Francisco.

Right: Second baseman Ray Durham donned a Sox uniform in 1995 and tied for sixth in the voting for American League Rookie of the Year. In '96 he led the team in doubles with 33 and in stolen bases, his 30 the sixth most in the American League. Durham's fielding average of .984 in 1996 was the fifth best in the league.

Left: After a brief appearance in 1995, James Baldwin earned a spot in the Sox regular rotation in 1996 and posted a record of 11-6 and an ERA of 4.42. He was named the American League's Rookie Pitcher of the Year by *The Sporting News*.

Above: Ron Karkovice broke in with the White Sox in 1986 and as a rookie that year caught Joe Cowley's no-hitter against the California Angels. His most productive year at the plate was 1989 when he hit .264, and in 1993 he contributed a career-high 20 home runs. Over his catching career, he has thrown out 39.3 percent (232 of 591) of those who have tried to steal bases on him, second highest among all current American League backstops.

Left: Jason Bere became a regular starter for the Sox as a rookie in 1993, and with a record of 12-5 and an ERA of 3.47 was runner-up for the American League Rookie of the Year award. The next year he posted a league-leading 12-2 record, a percentage of .857 which stands as the best in Sox history. In 1996 he made only five starts before undergoing season-ending elbow surgery.

Slugger Albert Belle joined the White Sox in 1997 after eight years with the Cleveland Indians. In 1996, Belle led the American League in RBIs with 148 and his 48 home runs ranked fourth; he also collected 187 hits (eighth best in the American League), 99 walks (seventh best) and scored 124 runs (sixth best), had 375 total bases (second best) and a slugging percentage of .623 (seventh best). (Photo courtesy of *Photography By Schuth*.)

In the modern era of White Sox lore, batters have hit three consecutive home runs in a single game four times.

May 28, 1995, vs. Detroit: Ray Durham, Ron Karkovice, Craig Grebeck
July 9, 1988, vs. Boston: Dan Pasqua, Greg Walker, Daryl Boston
August 24, 1985, vs. Toronto: Rudy Law, Bryan Little, Harold Baines
September 9, 1983, vs. California: Carlton Fisk, Tom Paciorek, Greg Luzinski

All four regular starters turned in winning seasons: Alex Fernandez, 16-10, Wilson Alvarez, 15-10, Kevin Tapani, 13-10, and James Baldwin, 11-6. Fernandez also registered the best ERA, 3.45, and Roberto Hernandez contributed 38 saves.

With the roller coaster on a climb, the Sox added superstar Albert Belle, formerly of the Cleveland Indians, to a powerhouse lineup for 1997, along with pitchers Jaime Navarro, Doug Drabek and reliever Roger McDowell.

Now, with the White Sox looking to their Diamond Jubilee at the close of the 20th century, and fielding one of the most imposing teams in club's history, there is reasonable and strong hope for a World Series to be hosted in the new Comiskey Park before the dawn of the 21st century.

In 1996, a new mark for "Home Run Trios" was set when Frank Thomas, Robin Ventura and Danny Tartabull combined to hammer 101 fourbaggers. Thomas had 40, Ventura 34, and Tartabull 27. Second on the all-time list, with a total of 93 homers is the 1983 trio of Ron Kittle, 35; Greg Luzinski, 32; and Carlton Fisk, 26.

Terry Bevington took over the managerial duties of the White Sox in June 1995 after serving as the Sox third base coach. He posted a record of 57-56 for the remainder of that season. In his first full season as manager, Bevington led the Sox to a second-place finish in the American League Central with a record of 85-77. Bevington was a catcher with the Milwaukee Brewers in the late 1970s and joined the White Sox coaching staff in 1989 after managerial positions with various minor league teams.

FRANK THOMAS' SIX YEARS WITH THE WHITE SOX

Year	Average	AB	Runs	Hits	HRs	RBIs
1991	.318	559	104	178	32	109
1992	.323	573	108	185	24	115
1993	.317	549	106	174	41	128
1994	.353	399	106	141	38	101
1995	.308	493	102	152	40	111
1996	.349	527	110	184	40	134

In 1995, Frank Thomas became just the second player in baseball history to hit a home run in each of the league's 14 different ballparks during a single season. Oakland's Ricky Henderson, in 1990, is the only other to have accomplished the feat.

Only four players in White Sox history have had seasons where they both batted over .300 and hit 25 home runs.

Frank Thomas accomplished it five times: 1991 (.318, 32), 1993 (.317, 41), 1994 (.353, 38), 1995 (.308, 40), 1996 (.349, 40).

Dick Allen did it twice: 1972 (.308, 37) and 1974 (.301, 32).

Harold Baines did it once: 1984 (.304, 29)

Zeke Bonura also did it once: 1934 (.302, 27).

Left: Jaime Navarro was acquired in 1997 to fill the void in the starting pitcher rotation after the departure of Alex Fernandez. Navarro moved crosstown from the Chicago Cubs where in the previous two years he won 29 games while losing 18. Prior to that, Navarro was 62-59 in six seasons with the Milwaukee Brewers.

Below: Chris Snopek took over at third base for the 1997 season after Robin Ventura broke his leg in spring training. Snopek was brought up from the minors in 1995. In 1996 he appeared in 46 games, batting .260 and hitting six home runs.

Nellie Fox

1950-1965
Hall of Fame 1997

In 1997, White Sox great Nellie Fox was finally inducted into baseball's Hall of Fame at Cooperstown, New York, as a selection of the Hall's Veterans Committee. The stellar second baseman for the Sox from 1950 to 1965 had long been in the running for baseball's highest recognition (he came within two votes in 1985, his 15th and final year of eligibility of baseball writers' balloting). It would be difficult to find a true White Sox fan who would disagree with Fox's close friend and former teammate Billy Pierce who said of the overdue honor: "It'll make a lot of people happy. If you look at some of the stats, it's amazing he wasn't in the Hall of Fame years ago."

Fox joined only 12 other second baseman enshrined in the Hall of Fame: Eddie Collins (A's, White Sox), Bobby Doerr (Red Sox), Johnny Evers (Cubs, Braves), Frankie Frisch (Giants, Cardinals), Charlie Gehringer (Tigers), Billy Herman (Cubs, Dodgers), Rogers Hornsby (Cardinals, Cubs), Nap Lajoie (Indians, Phillies), Tony Lazzeri (Yankees), Joe Morgan (Reds, Astros), Jackie Robinson (Dodgers) and Red Schoendienst (Cardinals, Braves).

Among the current 13 Hall of Fame second basemen, Fox posted the most 100-plus RBI seasons (7) and 100-plus runs-scored seasons (12), was named American League MVP once (1959) exceeded only by two-time MVP-winners Hornsby and Morgan, and his lifetime batting average of .288 is tied with Doerr for 10th best. His career fielding average of .984 is a major league record for a second baseman. Fox led the league's second basemen in fielding six times, second only to the seven registered by Collins and Gehringer. He played in 12 All-Star games, and was a starter in seven for the American League.

No one would have been happier to see Nellie Fox formally welcomed into the baseball Hall of Fame than famed-in-his-own-right poet, Ogden Nash who once penned these lines about the diminutive, tobacco-chaw-chewing second baseman...

Photo courtesy of the *National Baseball Hall of Fame Library, Cooperstown, NY and Wide World Photos.*

This holler guy who we are follering,
  what does he holler when he's hollering?
You can hear him clear to hell and gone,
  c'mon there baby, c'mon c'mon!

He uses a plug of tobacco per game,
  and has never lost or swallowed same.
Nellie Fox so lives to play,
  that every day's a hollerday.

Ogden Nash

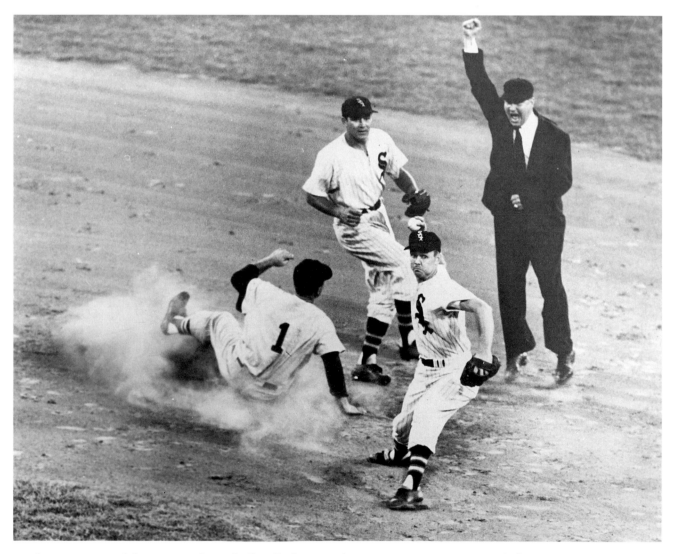

Photo courtesy of the *National Baseball Hall of Fame Library, Cooperstown, NY and The Bettmann Archive.*

Appendix
Statistics and Records

The Highest Honors

HALL OF FAME

Players	Years with the Sox
Eddie Collins	1915-26
Ed Walsh	1904-16
Ted Lyons	1923-42; 1946
Ray Schalk	1912-28
Luke Appling	1930-43; 1945-50
Red Faber	1914-33
Al Simmons	1933-35
Harry Hooper	1921-25
Early Wynn	1958-62
Luis Aparicio	1956-62; 1968-70
Hoyt Wilhelm	1963-68
Nellie Fox	1950-1965

Others	
Charles Comiskey, club owner	1901-31
Al Lopez, manager	1957-65; 1968-69
Bill Veeck, executive	1959-61; 1976-80

MOST VALUABLE PLAYER

Nellie Fox	1959
Dick Allen	1972
Frank Thomas	1993
Frank Thomas	1994

CY YOUNG AWARD WINNERS

Early Wynn	1959
LaMarr Hoyt	1983
Jack McDowell	1993

ROOKIES OF THE YEAR

Luis Aparicio	1956
Gary Peters	1963
Tommie Agee	1966
Ron Kittle	1983
Ozzie Guillen	1985

APPENDIX

ALL-TIME RECORDS
Individuals

<u>Batters</u>

Highest Batting Average
- Career: Shoeless Joe Jackson, .339
- Season: Luke Appling, .388 (1936)

Most At-Bats
- Career: Luke Appling, 8,856
- Season: Nellie Fox, 649 (1956)

Most Home Runs
- Career: Frank Thomas, 222
- Season: Frank Thomas, 41 (1993)
- Game: Pat Seerey, 4 (7/18/48, vs. Philadelphia)

Most Grand Slam Home Runs
- Career: Robin Ventura, 7
- Season: Pete Ward, 3 (1964)
- Game: Robin Ventura, 2 (9/4/95, vs. Texas)

Most Hits
- Career: Luke Appling, 2,749
- Season: Eddie Collins, 224 (1920)
- Game: Lance Johnson, 6 (9/23/95, vs. Minnesota)
  - Floyd Robinson, 6 (7/22/62, vs. Boston)
  - Hank Steinbacher, 6 (6/22/38, vs. Washington)
  - Rip Radcliff, 6 (7/13/36 vs. Philadelphia)

Most Runs
- Career: Luke Appling, 1,319
- Season: Johnny Mostil, 135 (1925)

Most RBIs
- Career: Luke Appling, 1,116
- Season: Zeke Bonura, 137 (1936)
- Game: RobinVentura, 8 (9/4/95, vs. Texas)
  - Jim Spencer, 8 (7/2/77, vs. Minnesota and 5/14/77 vs. Cleveland)
  - Tommy McCraw, 8 (5/24/67, vs. Minnesota)
  - Carl Reynolds, 8 (7/2/30, vs. New York)

Most Triples
- Career: Nellie Fox, 104
  - Shano Collins, 104
- Season: Shoeless Joe Jackson, 21 (1916)
- Game: Lance Johnson, 3 (9/23/95, vs. Minnesota)

Most Doubles
- Career: Luke Appling, 440
- Season: Frank Thomas, 46 (1992)
- Game: Marv Owen, 4 (4/23/39, vs. St. Louis)
  - Mike Kreevich, 4 (9/4/37, vs. Detroit)

Most Singles
    Career: Luke Appling, 2,162
    Season: Eddie Collins, 169 (1920)
Most Total Bases
    Career: Luke Appling, 3,528
    Season: Shoeless Joe Jackson, 336 (1920)
    Game: Pat Seerey, 16 (7/18/48, vs. Philadelphia)
Most Stolen Bases
    Career: Eddie Collins, 366
    Season: Rudy Law, 77 (1983)
    Game: Jimmy Callahan, 4 (9/16/05, vs. St. Louis)
               George Davis, 4 (6/14/05)
Most Bases on Balls
    Career: Luke Appling, 1,302
    Season: Frank Thomas, 138 (1991)
    Game: Tony Muser, 5 (7/3/73, vs. Texas)
               Frank Thomas, 5 (6/5/96 vs. Boston)
Highest Slugging Average
    Career: Frank Thomas, .599
    Season: Frank Thomas, .729 (1994)
Fewest Strikeouts
    Season: Nellie Fox, 11 (1951 & 1958)
Longest Hitting Streak:
               Luke Appling, 27 games (1936)

Pitchers

Most wins
    Career: Ted Lyons, 260
    Season: Ed Walsh, 40 (1908)
Most Shutouts
    Career: Ed Walsh, 57
    Season: Ed Walsh, 11 (1908)
Most Strikeouts
    Career: Billy Pierce, 1,796
    Season: Ed Walsh, 269 (1908)
    Game: Jack Harshman, 16 (7/25/54, vs. Boston)
Most Consecutive Strikeouts
               Joe Cowley, 7 (5/28/86, vs. Texas)
Most Games Pitched
    Career: Red Faber, 669
    Season: Wilbur Wood, 88 (1968)
Most Games Started
    Career: Red Faber, 484
               Ted Lyons, 484
    Season: Wilbur Wood, 49 (1972)
               Ed Walsh, 49 (1908)
Most Games Completed
    Career: Ted Lyons, 356
    Season: Ed Walsh, 42 (1908)

Most Innings Pitched
    Career: Ted Lyons, 4,161
    Season: Ed Walsh, 464 (1908)
Lowest ERA
    Career: Ed Walsh, 1.82
    Season: Ed Walsh, 1.27 (1910)
Highest Winning Percentage
    Career: Lefty Williams, .648 (81-44)
    Season: Jason Bere, .857 (12-2, 1994)
Most Seasons Winning 20 or More Games
    Wilbur Wood, 4
    Red Faber, 4
    Ed Walsh, 4
Most Consecutive Games Won
    Wilson Alvarez, 15 (1993-94)
    LaMarr Hoyt, 15 (1983-84)
Most Saves
    Career: Bobby Thigpen, 201
    Season: Bobby Thigpen, 57 (1990)
Most No-Hitters
    Frank Smith, 2 (9/20/08, vs. Philadelphia; 9/6/05, vs. Detroit)
Perfect Game
    Charles Robertson (4/30/22, vs. Detroit, 2-0)

Service

Most Seasons
    Batter: Luke Appling, 20
    Pitcher: Ted Lyons, 21
Most Games
    Batter: Luke Appling, 2,422
    Pitcher: Red Faber, 669

As a Team

Batting

Highest Batting Average	.295	(1920)
Most Home Runs	195	(1996)
Most Grand Slam homers	8	(1996)
Most Hits	1,597	(1936)
Most Runs	920	(1936)
Most RBIs	862	(1936)
Most Triples	102	(1915)
Most Doubles	314	(1926)
Most Singles	1,199	(1936)
Most .300 Hitters	5	(1920, 1924, 1936, 1937)
Most Stolen Bases	280	(1901)
Most Bases on Balls	702	(1949)
Highest Slugging Average	.447	(1996)

Pitching

Most Wins	100	(1917)
Most Shutouts	32	(1906)
Most Strikeouts	1,039	(1996)
Lowest ERA	1.99	(1905)
Most Saves	68	(1990)
Fewest Walks	255	(1906)

Fielding

Highest Average	.982	(1954, 1957, 1962, 1993, 1996)
Fewest Errors	107	(1957)
Most Consecutive Errorless Games	9	(1955, 1964, 1995)
Most Double Plays	188	(1974)

Yearly Leaders

Batting

Year	Batting Average (Min. 400 ABs)		Home Runs		Runs Batted In	
1901	F. Jones	.311	S. Mertes	5	S. Mertes	98
1902	F. Jones	.321	F. Isbell	4	G. Davis	93
1903	D. Green	.309	D. Green	6	D. Green	62
1904	D. Green	.265	F. Jones	3	G. Davis	69
1905	J. Donahue	.287	(3 players)	2	J. Donahue	76
1906	F. Isbell	.279	F. Jones	2	G. Davis	80
			B. Sullivan	2		
1907	P. Dougherty	.270	G. Rohe	2	J. Donahue	68
1908	P. Dougherty	.278	(4 players)	1	F. Jones	50
1909	P. Dougherty	.285	(3 players)	1	P. Dougherty	55
1910	P. Dougherty	.248	C. Gandil	2	P. Dougherty	43
1911	M. McIntyre	.323	P. Bodie	4	P. Bodie	97
			S. Collins	4		
1912	P. Bodie	.294	H. Lord	5	S. Collins	81
			P. Bodie	5		
1913	B. Weaver	.272	P. Bodie	8	B. Weaver	52
1914	S. Collins	.274	J. Fournier	6	S. Collins	65
1915	E. Collins	.332	J. Fournier	5	S. Collins	85
1916	J. Jackson	.341	H. Felsch	7	J. Jackson	78
1917	H. Felsch	.308	H. Felsch	6	H. Felsch	102
1918	B. Weaver	.300	E. Collins	2	S. Collins	56
1919	J. Jackson	.351	H. Felsch	7	J. Jackson	96
			J. Jackson	7		
1920	J. Jackson	.382	H. Felsch	14	J. Jackson	121
1921	E. Collins	.337	E. Sheely	11	E. Sheely	95
1922	E. Collins	.324	B. Falk	12	E. Sheely	80
					H. Hooper	80

Year	Batting Average		Home Runs		Runs Batted In	
1923	E. Collins	.360	H. Hooper	10	E. Sheely	88
1924	B. Falk	.352	H. Hooper	10	E. Sheely	103
1925	E. Collins	.346	E. Sheely	9	E. Sheely	111
1926	B. Falk	.345	B. Falk	8	B. Falk	108
1927	B. Falk	.327	B. Flak	9	W. Barrett	83
					B. Falk	83
1928	W. Kamm	.308	W. Barrett	3	W. Kamm	84
			A. Metzler	3		
1929	C. Reynolds	.317	C. Reynolds	11	C. Reynolds	67
1930	C. Reynolds	.359	C. Reynolds	22	S. Jolley	114
1931	L. Blue	.304	C. Reynolds	6	C. Reynolds	77
1932	B. Seeds	.290	R. Kress	9	L. Appling	63
1933	A. Simmons	.331	A. Simmons	14	A. Simons	119
1934	A. Simmons	.344	Z. Bonura	27	Z. Bonura	110
1935	L. Appling	.307	Z. Bonura	21	Z. Bonura	92
1936	L. Appling	.388	Z. Bonura	12	Z. Bonura	137
1937	Z. Bonura	.345	Z. Bonura	19	Z. Bonura	100
1938	R. Radcliff	.330	G. Walker	16	G. Walker	87
1939	E. McNair	.324	J. Kuhel	15	G. Walker	111
1940	L. Appling	.348	J. Kuhel	27	J. Kuhel	94
1941	T. Wright	.322	J. Kuhel	12	D. Wright	97
1942	D. Kolloway	.273	W. Moses	7	D. Kolloway	60
1943	L. Appling	.328	J. Kuhel	5	L. Appling	80
1944	R. Hodgin	.295	H. Trosky	10	H. Trosky	70
1945	T. Cuccinello	.308	J. Dickshot	4	R. Schalk	65
			G. Curtright	4		
1946	L. Appling	.309	T. Wright	7	L. Appling	55
1947	T. Wright	.324	R. York	15	R. York	64
1948	L. Appling	.314	P. Seerey	18	P. Seerey	64
1949	C. Michaels	.308	S. Souchock	7	C. Michaels	83
1950	E. Robinson	.314	G. Zernial	29	G. Zernial	93
1951	M. Minoso	.324	E. Robinson	29	E. Robinson	117
1952	N. Fox	.296	E. Robinson	22	E. Robinson	104
	E. Robinson	.296				
1953	M. Minoso	.313	M. Minoso	15	M. Minoso	104
1954	M. Minoso	.320	M. Minoso	19	M. Minoso	116
1955	G. Kell	.312	W. Dropo	19	G. Kell	81
1956	M. Minoso	.316	L. Doby	24	L. Doby	102
1957	N. Fox	.317	J. Rivera	14	M. Minoso	103
			L. Doby	14		
1958	N. Fox	.300	S. Lollar	20	S. Lollar	84
1959	N. Fox	.306	S. Lollar	22	S. Lollar	84
1960	A. Smith	.315	R. Sievers	28	M. Minoso	105
1961	F. Robinson	.310	A. Smith	28	A. Smith	93
1962	F. Robinson	.312	A. Smith	16	F. Robinson	109
1963	P. Ward	.295	P. Ward	22	P. Ward	84
			D. Nicholson	22		
1964	F. Robinson	.301	P. Ward	23	P. Ward	94
1965	D. Buford	.283	J. Romano	18	B. Skowron	78
			B. Skowron	18		

Year	Batting Average		Home Runs		Runs Batted In	
1966	T. Agee	.273	T. Agee	22	T. Agee	86
1967	D. Buford	.241	P. Ward	18	P. Ward	62
	K. Berry	.241				
1968	T. Davis	.268	P. Ward	15	P. Ward	50
					T. Davis	50
1969	W. Williams	.304	B. Melton	23	B. Melton	87
1970	L. Aparicio	.313	B. Melton	33	B. Melton	96
1971	C. May	.294	B. Melton	33	B. Melton	86
1972	R. Allen	.308	R. Allen	37	R. Allen	113
	C. May	.308				
1973	P. Kelly	.280	B. Melton	20	C. May	96
			C. May	20		
1974	J. Orta	.316	R. Allen	32	K. Hendersn	95
1975	J. Orta	.304	L. Johnson	18	J. Orta	83
1976	R. Garr	.300	J. Orta	14	J. Orta	72
			J. Spencer	14		
1977	R. Garr	.300	O. Gamble	31	R. Zisk	101
1978	R. Garr	.275	E. Soderholm	20	L. Johnson	72
1979	C. Lemon	.318	C. Lemon	17	C. Lemon	86
1980	C. Lemon	.292	J. Morrison	15	L. Johnson	81
			W. Nordhagen	15		
1981	W. Nordhagen	.308	G. Luzinski	21	G. Luzinski	61
1982	G. Luzinski	.292	H. Baines	25	H. Baines	105
1983	T. Paciorek	.307	R. Kittle	35	R. Kittle	100
1984	H. Baines	.304	R. Kittle	32	H. Baines	94
1985	H. Baines	.309	C. Fisk	37	H. Baines	113
1986	H. Baines	.296	H. Baines	21	H. Baines	88
1987	H. Baines	.293	I. Calderon	28	G. Walker	94
	I. Calderon	.293				
1988	H. Baines	.277	D. Pasqua	20	H. Baines	81
1989	I. Calderon	.286	I. Calderon	14	I. Calderon	87
1990	C. Fisk	.285	C. Fisk	18	I. Calderon	74
	L. Johnson	.285				
1991	F. Thomas	.318	F. Thomas	32	F. Thomas	109
1992	F. Thomas	.323	G. Bell	25	F. Thomas	115
1993	F. Thomas	.317	F. Thomas	41	F. Thomas	128
1994	F. Thomas	.353	F. Thomas	38	F. Thomas	101
1995	F. Thomas	.308	F. Thomas	40	F. Thomas	111
1996	F. Thomas	.349	F. Thomas	40	F. Thomas	134

Pitching

Year	Wins		Earned Run Average	
1901	C. Griffith	24-7	N. Callahan	2.42
1902	R. Patterson	19-14	N. Garvin	2.21
1903	D. White	17-16	D. White	2.13
1904	F. Owen	21-15	D. White	1.78

Year	Wins			Earned Run Average	
1905	N. Altrock	23-12		D. White	1.76
1906	F. Owen	22-13		D. White	1.52
1907	D. White	27-13		E. Walsh	1.60
1908	E. Walsh	40-15		E. Walsh	1.42
1909	F. Smith	25-17		E. Walsh	1.41
1910	E. Walsh	18-20		E. Walsh	1.27
1911	E. Walsh	27-18		E. Walsh	2.22
1912	E. Walsh	27-17		E. Walsh	2.15
1913	R. Russell	22-16		E. Cicotte	1.58
1914	J. Scott	14-18		E. Cicotte	2.04
	J. Fourvier	14-19			
1915	R. Faber	24-14		J. Scott	2.03
	J. Scott	24-11			
1916	R. Russell	18-11		E. Cicotte	1.78
1917	E. Cicotte	28-12		E. Cicotte	1.53
1918	E. Cicotte	12-19		J. Benz	2.51
1919	E. Cicotte	29-7		E. Cicotte	1.82
1920	R. Faber	23-13		R. Faber	2.99
1921	R. Faber	25-15		R. Faber	2.48
1922	R. Faber	21-17		R. Faber	2.80
1923	R. Faber	14-11		H. Thurston	3.05
1924	H. Thurston	20-14		H. Thurston	3.80
1925	T. Lyons	21-11		T. Blankenship	3.16
1926	T. Lyons	18-16		T. Lyons	3.01
1927	T. Lyons	22-14		T. Lyons	2.84
1928	T. Thomas	17-16		T. Thomas	3.08
1929	T. Thomas	14-18		T. Thomas	3.19
	T. Lyons	14-20			
1930	T. Lyons	22-15		T. Lyons	3.78
1931	V. Frasier	13-15		R. Faber	3.82
1932	T. Lyons	10-15		T. Lyons	3.28
	S. Jones	10-15			
1933	T. Lyons	10-21		S. Jones	3.36
	S. Jones	10-12			
	E. Durham	10-6			
1934	G. Earnshaw	14-11		G. Earnshaw	4.52
1935	T. Lyons	15-8		T. Lyons	3.02
1936	V. Kennedy	21-9		V. Kennedy	4.63
1937	M. Stratton	15-5		M. Stratton	2.40
1938	M. Stratton	15-9		T. Lee	3.49
1939	T. Lee	15-11		T. Lyons	2.76
	J. Rigney	15-8			
1940	E. Smith	14-9		J. Rigney	3.11
	J. Rigney	14-18			
1941	T. Lee	22-11		T. Lee	2.37
1942	T. Lyons	14-6		T. Lyons	2.10
1943	O. Grove	15-9		O. Grove	2.75
1944	B. Dietrich	16-17		J. Haynes	2.57
1945	T. Lee	15-12		T. Lee	2.44

Year	Wins		Earned Run Average	
1946	E. Lopat	13-13	E. Lopat	2.73
	E. Caldwell	13-4		1947
	E. Lopat	16-3	J. Haynes	2.42
1948	B. Wight	9-20	J. Haynes	3.97
	J. Haynes	9-10		
1949	B. Wight	15-13	B. Wight	3.31
1950	B. Pierce	12-16	B. Wight	3.58
1951	B. Pierce	15-14	S. Rogovin	2.48
1952	B. Pierce	15-12	J. Dobson	2.51
1953	B. Pierce	18-12	B. Pierce	2.72
1954	V. Trucks	19-12	S. Consuegra	2.69
1955	D. Donovan	15-9	B. Pierce	1.97
	B. Pierce	15-10		
1956	B. Pierce	20-9	J. Harshman	3.10
1957	B. Pierce	20-12	D. Donovan	2.77
1958	B. Pierce	17-11	B. Pierce	2.68
1959	E. Wynn	22-10	B. Shaw	2.69
1960	B. Pierce	14-7	F. Baumann	2.67
1961	J. Pizarro	14-7	J. Pizarro	3.05
1962	R. Herbert	20-9	E. Fisher	3.10
1963	G. Peters	19-8	G. Peters	2.33
1964	G. Peters	20-8	J. Horlen	1.88
1965	E. Fisher	15-7	E. Fisher	2.40
1966	T. John	14-11	H. Wilhelm	1.81
1967	J. Horlen	19-7	J. Horlen	2.06
1968	W. Wood	13-12	W. Wood	1.87
1969	J. Horlen	13-16	T. John	3.25
1970	T. John	12-17	T. John	3.28
1971	W. Wood	22-13	W. Wood	1.91
1972	W. Wood	24-17	W. Wood	2.51
1973	W. Wood	24-20	T. Forster	3.23
1974	J. Kaat	21-13	J. Kaat	2.92
1975	J. Kaat	20-14	J. Kaat	3.11
1976	K. Brett	10-12	K. Brett	3.32
1977	S. Stone	15-12	K. Kravec	4.10
1978	S. Stone	12-12	F. Barrios	4.05
1979	K. Kravec	15-13	R. Baumgarten	3.53
1980	B. Burns	15-13	B. Burns	2.84
1981	B. Burns	10-6	D. Lamp	2.41
1982	L. Hoyt	19-15	L. Hoyt	3.53
1983	L. Hoyt	24-10	R. Dotson	3.23
1984	T. Seaver	15-11	R. Dotson	3.59
1985	B. Burns	18-11	T. Seaver	3.17
1986	J. Crowley	11-11	F. Bannister	3.54
1987	F. Bannister	16-11	F. Bannister	3.58
1988	J. Reuss	13-9	D. LaPoint	3.40
1989	M. Perez	11-14	E. King	3.39
1990	G. Hibbard	14-9	G. Hibbard	3.16
	J. McDowell	14-9		

Year	Wins			Earned Run Average	
1991	J. McDowell	17-10		M. Perez	3.12
1992	J. McDowell	20-10		J. McDowell	3.18
1993	J. McDowell	22-10		W. Alvarez	2.95
1994	W. Alvarez	12-8		W. Alvarez	3.45
	J. Bere	12-2			
1995	A. Fernandez	12-8		A. Fernandez	3.80
1996	A. Fernandez	16-10		A. Fernandez	3.45

Year-By-Year Team Statistics

Year	Pos.	Won-Lost	Pct.	GA-GB	Manager	Attendance
1901	1	83-53	.610	4	Clark Griffith	354,350
1902	4	74-60	.552	8	Clark Griffith	337,898
1903	7	60-77	.438	30.5	James J. Callahan	286,183
1904	3	89-65	.578	6	Callahan-Fielder Jones	557,123
1905	2	92-60	.605	2	Fielder Jones	687,419
1906	1	93-58	.616	3	Fielder Jones	585,202
1907	3	87-64	.576	5.5	Fielder Jones	667,307
1908	3	88-64	.579	1.5	Fielder Jones	636,098
1909	4	78-74	.513	20	William J. Sullivan	475,400
1910	6	68-85	.444	35.5	Hugh Duffy	552,084
1911	4	77-74	.510	24	Hugh Duffy	583,208
1912	4	78-76	.506	28	James J. Callahan	602,241
1913	5	78-74	.513	17.5	James J. Callahan	644,501
1914	6	70-84	.455	30	James J. Callahan	469,290
1915	3	93-61	.604	9.5	Clarence Rowland	539,461
1916	2	89-64	.578	2	Clarence Rowland	679,923
1917	1	100-54	.679	9	Clarence Rowland	684,521
1918	6	57-67	.460	17	Clarence Rowland	195,081
1919	1	88-52	.629	3.5	William Gleason	627,186
1920	2	96-58	.623	2	William Gleason	833,492
1921	7	62-92	.403	36.5	William Gleason	543,650
1922	5	77-77	.500	17	William Gleason	602,860
1923	7	69-85	.448	30	William Gleason	573,778
1924	8	66-87	.431	25.5	Evers-Walsh-Collins-Evers	606,658
1925	5	79-75	.513	18.5	Eddie Collins	832,231
1926	5	81-72	.529	9.5	Eddie Collins	710,339
1927	5	70-83	.458	39.5	Ray W. Schalk	614,423
1928	5	72-82	.468	29	Schalk-Russ Blackburne	494,152
1929	7	59-93	.388	46	Russell Blackburne	426,795
1930	7	62-92	.403	40	Owen J. Bush	406,123
1931	8	56-97	.366	51.5	Owen J. Bush	403,550
1932	7	49-102	.325	56.5	Lewis A. Fonseca	233,198
1933	6	67-83	.447	31	Lewis A. Fonseca	397,789
1934	8	53-99	.349	47	Fonseca-James Dykes	236,559
1935	5	74-78	.487	19.5	James Dykes	470,281
1936	3	81-70	.536	20	James Dykes	440,810
1937	3	86-68	.558	16	James Dykes	589,245

Year	Pos.	Won-Lost	Pct.	GA-GB	Manager	Attendance
1938	6	65-83	.439	32	James Dykes	338,278
1939	4	85-69	.552	22.5	James Dykes	594,104
1940	4	82-72	.532	8	James Dykes	660,336
1941	3	77-77	.500	24	James Dykes	677,077
1942	6	66-82	.446	34	James Dykes	425,734
1943	4	82-72	.532	16	James Dykes	508,962
1944	7	71-83	.461	18	James Dykes	573,539
1945	6	71-78	.477	15	James Dykes	657,981
1946	5	74-80	.481	30	Dykes-Ted Lyons	983,403
1947	6	70-84	.455	27	Ted Lyons	876,948
1948	8	51-101	.336	44.5	Ted Lyons	777,844
1949	6	63-91	.409	34	Jack Onslow	937,151
1950	6	60-94	.390	38	Onslow-Corriden	781,330
1951	4	81-73	.526	17	Paul Richards	1,328,234
1952	3	81-73	.526	14	Paul Richards	1,231,675
1953	3	89-65	.578	11.5	Paul Richards	1,141,353
1954	3	94-60	.610	17	Richards-Marty Marion	1,231,629
1955	3	91-63	.591	5	Marty Marion	1,175,684
1956	3	85-69	.552	12	Marty Marion	1,000,090
1957	2	90-64	.584	8	Al Lopez	1,135,668
1958	2	82-72	.532	10	Al Lopez	797,451
1959	1	94-60	.610	5	Al Lopez	1,423,144
1960	3	87-67	.565	10	Al Lopez	1,644,460
1961	4	86-76	.531	23	Al Lopez	1,146,019
1962	5	85-77	.525	11	Al Lopez	1,131,562
1963	2	94-68	.580	10.5	Al Lopez	1,158,848
1964	2	98-64	.605	1	Al Lopez	1,250,053
1965	2	95-67	.586	7	Al Lopez	1,130,519
1966	4	83-79	.512	15	Eddie Stanky	990,016
1967	4	89-73	.549	3	Eddie Stanky	985,634
1968	8 tie	67-95	.414	36	Stanky-Moss-Lopez	803,775
1969	5	68-94	.420	29	Lopez-Gutteridge	589,546
1970	6	56-106	.346	42	Gutteridge-Adair-Tanner	495,355
1971	3	79-83	.488	22.5	Chuck Tanner	833,891
1972	2	87-67	.565	5.5	Chuck Tanner	1,186,018
1973	5	77-85	.475	17	Chuck Tanner	1,316,527
1974	4	80-80	.500	9	Chuck Tanner	1,163,596
1975	5	75-86	.466	22.5	Chuck Tanner	770,800
1976	6	64-97	.398	25.5	Paul Richards	914,945
1977	3	90-72	.556	12	Bob Lemon	1,657,135
1978	6	71-90	.441	20.5	Lemon-Larry Doby	1,491,100
1979	5	73-87	.456	14	Don Kessinger-LaRussa	1,280,702
1980	5	70-90	.438	26	Tony LaRussa	946,651
1981						
Pt. 1	3	31-22	.585	2.5	Tony LaRussa	946,651
Pt. 2	6	23-30	.434	7		
1982	3	87-75	.537	6	Tony LaRussa	1,567,787
1983	1	99-63	.611	20	Tony LaRussa	2,132,821
1984	5 tie	74-88	.457	10	Tony LaRussa	2,136,988

Year	Pos.	Won-Lost	Pct.	GA-GB	Manager	Attendance
1985	3	85-77	.525	6	Tony LaRussa	1,669,888
1986	5	72-90	.444	20	LaRussa-Rader-Fregosi	1,424,313
1987	5	77-85	.475	8	Jim Fregosi	1,208,060
1988	5	71-90	.441	32.5	Jim Fregosi	1,115,525
1989	7	69-92	.429	29.5	Jeff Torborg	1,045,651
1990	2	94-68	.580	9	Jeff Torborg	2,002,359
1991	2	87-75	.537	8	Jeff Torborg	2,934,154
1992	3	86-76	.531	10	Gene Lamont	2,681,156
1993	1	94-68	.580	8	Gene Lamont	2,581,091
1994	1	67-46	.593	1	Gene Lamont	1,697,398
1995	3	68-76	.472	32	Lamont-Terry Bevington	1,609,773
1996	2	85-77	.525	14.5	Terry Bevington	1,676,416

All-Time Top 10 Performers

Batters

Career

Batting Average

Shoeless Joe Jackson	.339
Eddie Collins	.331
Frank Thomas	.327
Carl Reynolds	.322
Zeke Bonura	.317
Bibb Falk	.315
Al Simmons	.315
Taffy Wright	.312
Luke Appling	.310
Rip Radcliff	.310

Hits

Luke Appling	2,749
Nellie Fox	2,470
Eddie Collins	2,007
Harold Baines	1,652
Luis Aparicio	1,576
Minnie Minoso	1,523
Ozzie Guillen	1,488
Ray Schalk	1,345
Buck Weaver	1,308
Carlton Fisk	1,259

Home Runs

Frank Thomas	222
Carlton Fisk	214
Harold Baines	208
Bill Melton	154
Robin Ventura	144
Ron Kittle	140
Minnie Minoso	135
Sherm Lollar	124
Greg Walker	113
Pete Ward	97

Triples

Shano Collins	104
Nellie Fox	104
Luke Appling	102
Eddie Collins	102
Johnny Mostil	82
Shoeless Joe Jackson	79
Minnie Minoso	79
Lance Johnson	77
Buck Weaver	69
Willie Kamm	67

Doubles		RBIs	
Luke Appling	440	Luke Appling	1,116
Nellie Fox	335	Harold Baines	914
Harold Baines	296	Minnie Minoso	808
Eddie Collins	266	Eddie Collins	804
Minnie Minoso	260	Carlton Fisk	762
Bibb Falk	245	Nellie Fox	740
Willie Kamm	243	Frank Thomas	729
Shano Collins	230	Sherm Lollar	631
Luis Aparicio	223	Bibb Falk	627
Carlton Fisk	214	Robin Ventura	624

Runs		Total Bases	
Luke Appling	1,319	Luke Appling	3,528
Nellie Fox	1,187	Nellie Fox	3,118
Eddie Collins	1,065	Harold Baines	2,660
Minnie Minoso	893	Eddie Collins	2,567
Luis Aparicio	791	Minnie Minoso	2,346
Harold Baines	741	Carlton Fisk	2,143
Fielder Jones	695	Luis Aparicio	2,036
Frank Thomas	675	Frank Thomas	1,970
Carlton Fisk	649	Shano Collins	1,740
Ozzie Guillen	634	Bibb Falk	1,714

Stolen Bases	
Eddie Collins	366
Luis Aparicio	318
Frank Isbell	250
Lance Johnson	226
Fielder Jones	206
Shano Collins	192
Luke Appling	179
Johnny Mostil	176
Ray Schalk	176
Buck Weaver	172

Single Season

Batting Average			Hits		
Luke Appling	.388	1936	Eddie Collins	224	1920
Shoeless Joe Jackson	.382	1920	Shoeless Joe Jackson	218	1920
Eddie Collins	.372	1920	Buck Weaver	208	1920
Eddie Collins	.360	1923	Rip Radcliff	207	1936
Carl Reynolds	.359	1930	Luke Appling	204	1936
Frank Thomas	.353	1994	Shoeless Joe Jackson	202	1916
Bibb Falk	.352	1924	Carl Reynolds	202	1930
Shoeless Joe Jackson	.351	1919	Nellie Fox	201	1954
Eddie Collins	.349	1924	Al Simmons	200	1933
Frank Thomas	.349	1996	Nellie Fox	198	1955
			Harold Baines	198	1985

Home Runs

Frank Thomas	41	1993
Frank Thomas	40	1995
Frank Thomas	40	1996
Frank Thomas	38	1994
Dick Allen	37	1972
Carlton Fisk	37	1985
Ron Kittle	35	1983
Bill Melton	33	1970
Bill Melton	33	1971
Dick Allen	32	1974
Greg Luzinski	32	1983
Ron Kittle	32	1984
Frank Thomas	32	1991

Triples

Shoeless Joe Jackson	21	1916
Shoeless Joe Jackson	20	1920
Harry Lord	18	1911
Jack Fournier	18	1915
Carl Reynolds	18	1930
Minnie Minoso	18	1954
Sam Mertes	17	1901
Shano Collins	17	1915
Shoeless Joe Jackson	17	1917

Doubles

Frank Thomas	46	1992
Floyd Robinson	45	1962
Ivan Calderon	44	1990
Chet Lemon	44	1979
Earl Sheely	43	1925
Bibb Falk	43	1926
Shoeless Joe Jackson	42	1920
Red Kress	42	1932
Luke Appling	42	1937
Johnny Mostil	41	1926
Zeke Bonura	41	1937

RBIs

Zeke Bonura	137	1936
Frank Thomas	134	1996
Luke Appling	128	1936
Frank Thomas	128	1993
Shoeless Joe Jackson	121	1920
Al Simmons	119	1933
Eddie Robinson	117	1951
Minnie Minoso	116	1954
Happy Felsch	115	1920
Frank Thomas	115	1992

Runs

Johnny Mostil	135	1925
Fielder Jones	120	1901
Johnny Mostil	120	1926
Zeke Bonura	120	1936
Rip Radcliff	120	1936
Lu Blue	119	1931
Minnie Minoso	119	1954
Tony Phillips	119	1996
Eddie Collins	118	1915
Eddie Collins	117	1920

Total Bases

Shoeless Joe Jackson	336	1920
Frank Thomas	333	1993
Frank Thomas	330	1996
Carl Reynolds	329	1930
Frank Thomas	309	1991
Harold Baines	308	1984
Frank Thomas	307	1992
Dick Allen	305	1972
Robin Ventura	305	1996
Minnie Minoso	304	1954

Stolen Bases

Rudy Law	77	1983
Wally Moses	56	1943
Luis Aparicio	56	1959
Eddie Collins	53	1917
Luis Aparicio	53	1961
Frank Isbell	52	1901
Gary Redus	52	1987
Luis Aparicio	51	1960
Don Buford	51	1966
Tim Raines	51	1991

Pitchers

<u>Career</u>

Most Wins

Ted Lyons	260
Red Faber	254
Ed Walsh	195
Billy Pierce	186
Wilbur Wood	163
Doc White	159
Ed Cicotte	156
Joel Horlen	113
Frank Smith	108
Jim Scott	107

ERA

Ed Walsh	1.82
Frank Smith	2.18
Ed Cicotte	2.24
Doc White	2.30
Jim Scott	2.32
Reb Russell	2.34
Nick Altrock	2.40
Joe Benz	2.42
Frank Owen	2.48
Roy Patterson	2.75

Strikeouts

Billy Pierce	1,796
Ed Walsh	1,732
Red Faber	1,471
Gary Peters	1,341
Wilbur Wood	1,332
Ted Lyons	1,073
Doc White	1,067
Joel Horlen	1,007
Ed Cicotte	961
Jim Scott	945

Shutouts

Ed Walsh	57
Doc White	43
Billy Pierce	35
Red Faber	30
Ed Cicotte	28
Ted Lyons	27
Jim Scott	26
Frank Smith	25
Reb Russell	24
Wilbur Wood	24

<u>Winning Percentage</u>

Lefty Williams	.648
Juan Pizarro	.615
Jack McDowell	.611
Dickie Kerr	.609
Ed Walsh	.609
Ed Cicotte	.608
LaMarr Hoyt	.602
Dick Donovan	.593
Eddie Fisher	.575
Frank Smith	.574

Saves

Bobby Thigpen	201
Roberto Hernandez	134
Hoyt Wilhelm	98
Terry Forster	75
Wilbur Wood	57
Bob James	56
Ed Farmer	54
Clint Brown	53
Bob Locker	48
Turk Lown	45

Single Season

Wins

Ed Walsh	40	1908
Ed Cicotte	29	1919
Ed Cicotte	28	1917
Doc White	27	1907
Ed Walsh	27	1911
Ed Walsh	27	1912
Frank Smith	25	1909
Red Faber	25	1921
Clark Griffith	24	1901
Ed Walsh	24	1907
Jim Scott	24	1915
Red Faber	24	1915
Wilbur Wood	24	1972
Wilbur Wood	24	1973
LaMarr Hoyt	24	1983

ERA

Ed Walsh	1.27	1910
Ed Walsh	1.41	1909
Ed Walsh	1.42	1908
Doc White	1.52	1906
Ed Cicotte	1.53	1917
Ed Cicotte	1.58	1913
Ed Walsh	1.60	1907
Doc White	1.78	1904
Doc White	1.72	1909
Doc White	1.76	1905

Strikeouts

Ed Walsh	269	1908
Ed Walsh	258	1910
Ed Walsh	255	1911
Ed Walsh	254	1912
Gary Peters	215	1967
Wilbur Wood	210	1971
Tom Bradley	209	1972
Ed Walsh	206	1907
Tom Bradley	206	1971
Gary Peters	205	1964

Shutouts

Ed Walsh	11	1908
Ed Walsh	10	1906
Ed Walsh	8	1909
Reb Russell	8	1913
Wilbur Wood	8	1972
Doc White	7	1904
Doc White	7	1906
Doc White	7	1907
Frank Smith	7	1909
Ed Walsh	7	1910
Jim Scott	7	1915
Ed Cicotte	7	1917
Billy Pierce	7	1953
Ray Herbert	7	1963
Wilbur Wood	7	1971

Winning Percentage

Jason Bere	.857	1994
Sandy Consuegra	.842	1954
Ed Cicotte	.806	1919
Clark Griffith	.774	1901
Rich Dotson	.759	1983
Doc White	.750	1906
Monty Stratton	.750	1937
Bob Shaw	.750	1959
Joel Horlen	.731	1967
Ed Walsh	.727	1908
Dick Donovan	.727	1957

Saves

Bobby Thigpen	57	1990
Roberto Hernandez	38	1993
Roberto Hernandez	38	1996
Bobby Thigpen	34	1988
Bobby Thigpen	34	1989
Bob James	32	1985
Roberto Hernandez	32	1995
Ed Farmer	30	1980
Bobby Thigpen	30	1991
Terry Forster	29	1972
Hoyt Wilhelm	27	1964

Manager Records

Most Wins

Manager	Wins	(Losses)	Years
Jimmy Dykes	899	(940)	1935-46
Al Lopez	840	(650)	1957-65, 68-69
Tony LaRussa	522	(510)	1979-86
Fielder Jones	426	(293)	1904-08
Paul Richards	406	(362)	1951-54, 76
Chuck Tanner	401	(414)	1970-75
Kid Gleason	392	(364)	1919-23
Clarence Rowland	339	(247)	1915-18
Nixey Callahan	309	(329)	1903-04, 12-14
Gene Lamont	258	(210)	1992-95
Jeff Torborg	250	(235)	1989-91

Best Percentage

Manager	Pct.	Won-Lost	Years
Clark Griffith	.581	157-113	1901-02
Clarence Rowland	.578	339-247	1915-18
Fielder Jones	.576	426-293	1904-08
Marty Marion	.565	179-138	1954-56
Al Lopez	.562	840-650	1957-65, 68-69
Gene Lamont	.551	258-210	1992-95
Paul Richards	.529	406-362	1951-54, 76
Bob Lemon	.525	124-112	1977-78
Eddie Collins	.521	174-160	1924-26
Kid Gleason	.519	392-364	1919-23

Retired Jersey Numbers

2	Nellie Fox, 2B	(1950-63)
3	Harold Baines, OF	(1980-89, 96-)
4	Luke Appling, SS	(1930-50)
9	Minnie Minoso, OF	(1951-57, 60-61, 64, 76, 80)
11	Luis Aparicio, SS	(1956-62, 68-70)
16	Ted Lyons, P	(1923-42, 46)
19	Billy Pierce, P	(1949-61)

No-Hitters

Pitcher	Date	Opponent	Score (Sox-Opp.)
Nixey Callahan	9/20/02	Detroit	3-0
Frank Smith	9/6/05	Detroit	15-0
Frank Smith	9/20/08	Philadelphia	1-0
Ed Walsh	8/27/11	Boston	5-0
Joe Benz	5/31/14	Cleveland	6-1
Ed Cicotte	4/14/17	St. Louis	11-0
Charles Robertson	4/30/22	Detroit	2-0
Ted Lyons	8/21/26	Boston	6-0
Vern Kennedy	8/31/35	Cleveland	5-0
Bill Dietrich	6/1/37	St. Louis	8-0
Bob Keegan	8/20/57	Washington	6-0
Joel Horlen	9/10/67	Detroit	6-0
John Odom	9/10/67	Detroit	6-0
Francisco Barrios	7/28/76	Oakland	2-1
Joe Cowley	9/19/86	California	7-1
Wilson Alvarez	8/11/91	Baltimore	7-0

Gold Glove Awards (Fielding)

1957	Nellie Fox, 2B	1963	Jim Landis, OF
	Sherm Lollar, C	1964	Jim Landis, OF
	Minnie Minoso, OF	1966	Tommy Agee, OF
1958	Luis Aparicio, SS	1968	Luis Aparicio, SS
	Sherm Lollar, C	1970	Luis Aparicio, SS
1959	Luis Aparicio, SS		Ken Berry, OF
	Nellie Fox, 2B	1973	Jim Kaat, P
	Sherm Lollar, C	1974	Jim Kaat, P
1960	Luis Aparicio, SS	1975	Jim Kaat, P
	Nellie Fox, 2B	1977	Jim Spencer, 1B
	Minnie Minoso, OF	1981	Mike Squires, 1B
	Jim Landis, OF	1990	Ozzie Guillen, SS
1961	Luis Aparicio, SS	1991	Robin Ventura, 3B
	Jim Landis, OF	1992	Robin Ventura, 3B
	Earl Battey, C	1993	Robin Ventura, 3B
1962	Luis Aparicio, SS	1996	Robin Ventura, 3B
	Jim Landis, OF		

All-Star Game Selections
(Bold Type indicates starters)

1933 **Al Simmons, OF**; Jimmy Dykes, 3B

1934 **Al Simmons, OF**; Jimmy Dykes, 3B

1935 **Al Simmons, OF**

1936 **Luke Appling, SS; Rip Radcliff, OF**; Vern Kennedy, P

1937 Luke Sewell, C; Monty Stratton, P

1938 **Mike Kreevich, OF**

1939 Luke Appling, SS; Ted Lyons, P

1940 **Luke Appling, SS**

1941 Luke Appling, SS; Thornton Lee, P; Edgar Smith, P

1942 Edgar Smith, P

1943 Luke Appling, SS

1944 **Thurman Tucker, OF**; Orval Grove, P

1946 Luke Appling, SS

1947 Luke Appling, SS; Rudy York, 1B

1948 Joe Haynes, P

1949 **Cass Michaels, 2B**

1950 Rae Scarborough, P

1951 **Chico Carrasquel, SS; Nellie Fox, 2B**; Jim Busby, OF; Randy Gumpert, P; Minnie Minoso, OF; Eddie Robinson, 1B

1952 **Eddie Robinson, 1B**; Nellie Fox, 2B; Minnie Minoso, OF

1953 **Chico Carrasquel, SS; Billy Pierce, P**; Ferris Fain, 1B; Nellie Fox, 2B; Minnie Minoso, OF

1954 **Chico Carrasquel, SS; Minnie Minoso, OF**; Sandy Consuegra, P; Ferris Fain, 1B; Nellie Fox, 2B; Bob Keegan, P; George Kell, 3B; Sherm Lollar, C; Virgil Trucks, P

1955 **Nellie Fox, 2B; Billy Pierce, P**; Chico Carrasquel, SS; Dick Donovan, P; Sherm Lollar, C

1956 **Nellie Fox, 2B; Billy Pierce, P**; Sherm Lollar, C; Jim Wilson, P

1957 **Nellie Fox, 2B**; Minnie Minoso, OF; Billy Pierce, P

1958 **Luis Aparicio, SS; Nellie Fox, 2B**; Sherm Lollar, C; Billy Pierce, P; Early Wynn, P

1959 **Luis Aparicio, SS; Nellie Fox, 2B; Early Wynn, P**; Sherm Lollar, C; Billy Pierce, P

1960 **Minnie Minoso, OF**; Luis Aparicio, SS; Nellie Fox, 2B; Sherm Lollar, C; Al Smith, OF; Gerry Staley, P; Early Wynn, P

1961 Luis Aparicio, SS; Nellie Fox, 2B; Ray Herbert, P; Billy Pierce, P; Roy Sievers, 1B

1962 **Luis Aparicio, SS**; Jim Landis, OF

1963 **Nellie Fox, 2B**: Juan Pizarro, P

1964 Gary Peters, P; Juan Pizarro, P

1965 Eddie Fisher, P; Bill Skowron, 1B

1966 Tommy Agee, OF

1967 Tommy Agee, OF; Ken Berry, OF; Joel Horlen, P; Gary Peters, P

1968 Tommy John, P; Duane Josephson, C

1969 Carlos May, OF

1970 **Luis Aparicio, SS**

1971 Bill Melton, 3B

1972 **Dick Allen, 1B**; Carlos May, OF; Wilbur Wood, P

1973 **Dick Allen, 1B**; Pat Kelly, OF

1974 **Dick Allen, 1B**; Ed Herrmann, C; Wilbur Wood, P
1975 Bucky Dent, SS; Rich Gossage, P; Jim Kaat, P; Jorge Orta, 2B
1976 Rich Gossage, P
1977 **Richie Zisk, OF**
1978 Chet Lemon, OF
1979 Chet Lemon, OF
1980 Ed Farmer, P
1981 **Carlton Fisk, C**; Britt Burns, P
1982 **Carlton Fisk, C**
1983 Ron Kittle, OF
1984 Rich Dotson, P.
1985 **Carlton Fisk, C**; Harold Baines, OF
1986 Harold Baines, OF
1987 Harold Baines, OF
1988 Ozzie Guillen, SS
1989 **Harold Baines, DH**
1990 Ozzie Guillen, SS; Bobby Thigpen, P
1991 Carlton Fisk, C; Ozzie Guillen, SS; Jack McDowell, P
1992 Jack McDowell, P; Robin Ventura, 3B
1993 Jack McDowell, P; Frank Thomas, 1B
1994 **Frank Thomas, 1B**; Wilson Alvarez, P; Jason Bere, P
1995 **Frank Thomas, 1B**
1996 **Frank Thomas, 1B**; Roberto Hernandez, P

Index

(Names in bold are
White Sox players, coaches
or personnel.)

INDEX